The Gourmet Gardener

The Garden Club of Kentucky, Inc.

Internation Standard Book Number 0-913383 50 3
Library of Congress Catalog Card Number 97-065266

Cover design and book layout by James Asher Graphics

Front cover water color art by Vicki Jody

Manufactured in the United States of America

All book order correspondence should be addressed to:

The Garden Club of Kentucky, Inc.
960 Maple Grove Road
London, KY 40744

Commonwealth Book Company
Kuttawa, Kentucky

ACKNOWLEDGEMENTS

Sincere appreciation is extended to all who contributed to this cookbook. Special thanks are due to the committee who worked so diligently, reading, sorting, typing and even testing.

Mrs. R. Springer Hoskins, General Chairman
The Garden Club of Kentucky, Inc., President

Mrs. William Robinson, Co-Chairman
Lady Slipper Garden Club, Laurel Garden Club

Mrs. Denton Fuson, Selection Chairman
Corbin Garden Club

Mrs. Sam Scott, Organization Chairman
Lady Slipper Garden Club

Mrs. Edward Breining
Cumberland Park Garden Club

Mrs. Charles Huddleston
Cumberland Park Garden Club

Mrs. Paul Smith
Cumberland Falls Garden Club

Miss Margie Stephens
Cumberland Falls Garden Club

Mrs. Bill Young
Corbin Garden Club

ABOUT THE ARTIST

Vicki Jody was born and reared in Kentucky. She studied art in high school in Ohio under her brother, Byron Jody.

She has a Bachelors degree in art from Cumberland College. She also has a Para-professional Librarian Certificate and is presently the Director of the Corbin Public Library.

INTRODUCTION

Anyone who has ever visited Kentucky knows the hospitality that is our way of life. Folks here love to entertain and to be entertained. And so, we are always on the lookout for new ideas.

Knowing that every part of the country has its own specialty, we invited Garden Club Presidents around the country to participate in this book. It contains menu suggestions using favorite recipes.

The book is divided into three parts. "The Presidents Pick" starts out with a favorite menu from our National President. The country is divided into eight regions. Kentucky is in the region known as South Atlantic and our Director has contributed. Following those are menus and recipes from several State Presidents.

The second section, "The Sideboard", contains menus with recipes from members of the Board of Directors and other club members in Kentucky.

Some Garden Club members combined their ideas and submitted menus. You'll find they are "Too Good to Miss" in section three.

It is our hope that as you travel through this book you will find a taste of the nation's Gourmet Gardeners mixed with Kentucky hospitality.

Anne Hoskins, President
The Garden Club of Kentucky, Inc.
1995-1997

Nannine Clay Wallis House
State Headquarters
The Garden Club of Kentucky, Inc.
616 Pleasant Street
Paris, Kentucky

HISTORY

The headquarters of The Garden Club of Kentucky, Inc. is located at 616 Pleasant St., Paris, Kentucky. It is an old home with a spacious lawn and gardens. It was left in trust to the Garden Club by Mrs. Nannine Clay Wallis in 1970 with the provision it be used as headquarters for a period of thirty years.

Mrs. Wallis is one of the founders of The Garden Club of Kentucky, having served as president 1933-1935. She was also a Regional Director and The National Council of State Garden Clubs President 1939-1941.

Over the years, the Garden Club has maintained this property with the aid of a trust fund, grants and donations from clubs and members.

The grounds include one of the finest old tree collections in Central Kentucky and a conifer garden is planned with several trees already in place.

There is a small water garden with gold fish, a butterfly garden, two rose gardens, a day lily garden and other plantings in the yard.

A carriage house in the rear has been restored along with a trellis and pergola. A recent Eagle Scout project is the planting of an herb garden with labels in braille.

A nursery on the grounds, made possible by a grant from The National Tree Trust, Washington, D.C., houses tree seedlings. These will be pot grown until large enough to be donated for community plantings.

A study guide is available to visitors and tours can be arranged by appointment [(606)987-6158].

The PRESIDENTS PICK

Menus from the National President,
Regional Director
and
State Presidents

My Mother's Rice & Cheese Casserole

1 c. long grain rice, not washed
1/3 c. shortening
2 T. flour, heaping full
Few grains salt
Milk
1 small pkg. Velveeta Cheese
1/2 stick butter

Cook rice according to directions on box; blanch in cold water. In saucepan, melt shortening; add flour and salt. Add milk to almost top of small pan, stirring constantly until thickened. Cut cheese into small pieces and put in deep 10" casserole. Add rice and white sauce. Mix well; dot with butter. Bake 30-45 minutes at 350. Don't overbake; should have a nice creamy color on top.

Orange-Spinach Salad

1 10 oz. bag spinach
1 medium head lettuce, shredded
2 T. or more onion, diced; or purple onion, sliced
2 T. green pepper, diced
2 T. pimiento, diced
2 large oranges, peeled and chopped
1 small cucumber, sliced

Wash and tear spinach and lettuce and chill. Add remaining ingredients at last minute, and toss with dressing. Can be garnished with sliced hard boiled eggs, chopped crisp bacon and/or toasted almond slices.

Honey Caraway Dressing

3/4 c. mayonnaise
1 T. lemon juice
2 T. honey
1 T. caraway seed

In a small bowl, with wire whisk or fork, stir ingredients until blended.

Never Fail Butter Rolls

1-1/2 c. milk
1 c. sugar
1/2 c. warm water
2 pkgs. dry yeast
3 c. flour
2 sticks butter
4 eggs
1 t. salt
4 or more c. flour

Bring milk just to a boil. Pour over sugar, stirring well. Cool. Mix warm water with yeast. Add to milk and sugar. Beat in 3 cups flour. Let rise 1 hour. Melt butter and beat well with eggs and salt. Add to dough. Add remaining flour, mixing well. Cover and let rise until double. Punch down and put in refrigerator. Roll out on floured board, form into rolls and put on cookie sheet or put two rolls in each muffin tin; let rise. Before placing in oven, brush with melted butter. Bake at 350 for 10-15 minutes or until lightly browned.

Uncooked Lemon Pie

1 box vanilla wafers
3 egg yolks
1 can sweetened condensed milk
1 T. grated lemon rind (optional)
Juice of 2 lemons
3 egg whites
1/4 t. cream of tartar
6 T. sugar

Edge pie plate with vanilla wafers and cover bottom of plate with wafer crumbs; set aside. Beat egg yolks until thick and lemon colored. Add milk slowly and continue beating. Add rind, if using, and lemon juice. Pour into pie plate. Beat egg whites with cream of tartar until stiff enough to hold a point, then gradually beat in the sugar, continuing to beat until the mixture is stiff and glossy. Pile lightly on the pie filling, being sure the meringue completely covers the custard. Bake 15-20 minutes at 300, watching closely.

Seafood Dinner

M E N U

Mrs. Myles W. Whitlock, Jr., Director
South Atlantic Region
Seafood Combo*
Salad
Hard Rolls
Caribbean Fudge Pie*

Seafood Combo

1 28 oz. can crushed tomatoes
1/2 c. dry white wine
1/2 c. chopped parsley
2 T. olive oil
3 garlic cloves, crushed
1 t. salt
1/2 t. dried basil
1/4 t. fresh ground pepper
1/2 lb. halibut, cut into chunks
1 lb. shrimp, shelled and deveined
1 lb. sea scallops, cut in half if very large
1/2 c. ripe olives, pitted and sliced
12 oz. cooked linguine or spaghetti
1/3 c. fresh parmesan cheese, grated

In a large pot, combine first 8 ingredients; simmer uncovered for 20 minutes. Add fish, cook 5 more minutes. Add shrimp and scallops; cook 2-3 more minutes. Stir in olives. Serve over pasta and sprinkle with cheese.

Caribbean Fudge Pie

1/4 c. butter
3/4 c. brown sugar
3 eggs
1 12 oz. pkg. semi-sweet chocolate pieces, melted
2 t. instant coffee
1 t. rum extract
1/4 c. all purpose flour
1 c. chopped walnuts
1 9" unbaked pie shell
Whipped cream

Cream butter and sugar; beat in eggs one at a time. Add melted chocolate, coffee and rum. Stir in flour and walnuts. Pour into pie shell. Bake at 375 for 25 minutes. Cool. Serve at room temperature with whipped cream.

All Alaska Dinner

M E ❧ N U

Roberta Rice, President
Alaska Federation of Garden Clubs

Baked Salmon* Buttered New Potatoes
Broccoli Vegetable Relish Tray
Cranberry Muffins* Blueberry Cream Pie*

Baked Salmon

4-5 lb. roast king or red salmon

Wrap in foil; bake 1-1/2 hours at 400.

Cranberry Muffins

3/4 c. lingonberries (high bush cranberries)
1/2 c. confectioner's sugar
2 c. flour
3 t. baking powder
1 t. salt
1/4 c. sugar
1 egg
1 c. milk
1/4 c. oil

Mix berries with confectioner's sugar; set aside. In medium bowl mix flour, baking powder, salt and sugar. Add eggs, milk and oil. Stir until flour mixture is damp. Fold in sugared berries. Fill greased muffin tins 2/3 full. Bake 25 minutes at 350. Serve immediately with butter.

Blueberry Cream Pie

1 c. flour
1/3 c. shortening
1/4 t. salt
4 t. cold water
3 c. fresh Alaska wild blueberries, sprinkled with sugar
2/3 c. sugar
1/2 t. salt
3-1/2 T. cornstarch
3 c. skimmed milk
3 egg yolks
1 t. vanilla
1 T. butter
Whipped cream, if desired

Mix flour, shortening and salt until they resemble a coarse meal. Add water, 1 tablespoon at a time, stirring lightly until mixture forms a ball. Roll out on floured board. Position in 9" pie dish. Prick with fork and flute edge. Bake 8-10 minutes at 400. In saucepan mix together sugar, salt, cornstarch and milk. Cook gently until thickened. Boil one minute. Beat egg yolks and stir some of the hot mixture into egg yolks. Add to pan and mix in vanilla and butter. Boil 1 minute. Cool slightly. Pour 1/2 the blueberries into cooled crust. Pour cooled custard on top. Stir gently without breaking berries. Pour remaining berries on top. Chill 2 hours or more. Serve with whipped cream, slightly sweetened, if desired.

Mexican Patio Dinner

M E ❧ N U

Bunny Gladhart, President
Arizona Federation of Garden Clubs, Inc.

Classic Guacamole	Roasted Tomato &
Pepper Salsa	Tacos
Fajitas*	Southwest Rice
Grilled Corn	Lime Sorbet

Fajitas

2 lb. flank steak, cut against the grain in 1/4" x 2" strips
2 tomatoes, sliced in wedges
3 bell peppers
1-2 Spanish onions
1 dozen flour tortillas
2 limes

Marinade:
1 c. pineapple juice
1 c. soy sauce
1 T. garlic powder
1 t. black pepper

Pico de Gallo Salsa:
2 tomatoes, diced
2 jalapeño peppers, roasted, peeled and diced
1 bunch cilantro
1 small white onion, diced
1 clove garlic, minced
1 31 oz. can refried beans
Garlic, tabasco and chili powder (optional)

In a plastic zipper bag, mix the marinade. Marinate the meat for 5 minutes, drain and set aside. Slice the peppers and onion into 1/4" rings and set aside. Roll the individual flour tortillas in foil and place in a double boiler or steamer to warm, at least 30 minutes. Quarter the limes and set aside. Prepare the guacamole and Pico de Gallo Salsa. Heat the refried beans in a skillet, thoroughly, adding boiling water if they become too thick. At this point you may add a little garlic, tabasco and chili powder to taste. When everything else is ready, add a small amount of oil to a pan and sauté the meat, peppers and onions for 3 to 4 minutes. To serve, present in a series of bowls or plates the warm flour tortillas still in the foil, Pico de Gallo Salsa, guacamole, warm refried beans, fajita (meat) mixture garnished with tomato wedges and the lime wedges. Everyone can build their own meal in the warm flour tortillas.

Catfish Dinner

M E N U

Jeanette T. Golden, President
Arkansas Federation of Garden Clubs, Inc.

Catfish Dinner*	French Fries
Hush Puppies*	Cole Slaw
Banana Pudding	

Catfish Dinner

2 c. yellow cornmeal
3 T. salt
2 T. black pepper
3 T. red pepper
Catfish fillets, 2-3 per person
Oil for frying

Mix cornmeal, salt and peppers together. Roll fish in mixture until well coated. Drop into oil that has been heated to 350. Cook until golden brown and floats in the oil.

Hush Puppies

2 c. cornmeal
1 c. flour
2 eggs, beaten
3 t. baking powder
1-1/2 t. salt
1 small can cream style corn
3 jalapeño peppers, chopped
1/4 bell pepper, chopped
1 small onion, minced
Pinch of baking soda
Buttermilk

Mix all ingredients together, adding enough buttermilk to make the batter the consistency of cornbread batter. Fry these in the oil in which the fish has been cooked.

"California"
Simple, But Delicious

M E ❧ N U

Peggy Northon, President
California Garden Clubs, Inc.

Sangria*
Mexican Tortilla Casserole*
Mixed Green Salad
Next Best Thing to Robert Redford Dessert*

Sangria

1 liter red wine
1/4 c. brandy
1/8 c. Cointreau
1/2 liter soda water
1/4 peach, chopped
1 peach stone
1 banana, sliced
1 large lemon, cut into 8 pieces
Pinch cinnamon

Mix all of the ingredients together in a large pitcher. Refrigerate at least 24 hours. Add a little sugar if you wish.

Mexican Tortilla Casserole

1-1/2 lb. ground beef
1 pkg. spaghetti sauce mix
1 pkg. chili seasoning
1 8 oz. can tomato sauce
1 16 oz. can tomatoes
6 tortillas
1 small can green chili peppers, diced
12 oz. Jack cheese, grated

Sauté meat until lightly browned in a large skillet. Make spaghetti sauce according to package directions. Add chili seasoning, tomato sauce and tomatoes; add to meat. Cut tortillas in quarters. In medium sized, buttered casserole, layer tortillas, sauce, Jack cheese and chili peppers. Bake in 350 oven for 40 minutes.

Next Best Thing to Robert Redford Dessert

1 stick margarine or butter, melted
1 c. flour
1/2 to 1 c. chopped pecans
1 c. sugar
1 8 oz. cream cheese
12 oz. container Cool Whip, divided
1 large pkg. instant chocolate pudding
1 large pkg. instant vanilla pudding
3 c. milk
Grated chocolate

Mix together margarine, flour and pecans. Pat into a 9x13" baking pan. Bake at 350 for 15-20 minutes. Cool. Beat sugar and cream cheese together. Fold in 1/2 of the Cool Whip; spread over crust. Beat pudding mixes and milk together and spread over cream cheese mixture. Top with remaining Cool Whip and garnish with grated chocolate

Mongol Soup

1 can tomato soup
1 can smooth pea soup
2 cans water
1 large bay leaf
Sprinkle of fresh basil
Large dash of sherry

Mix all ingredients together in saucepan and heat.

Susan's Simple Chicken Salad

Olive or safflower oil
4 chicken breasts, boned and skinned
1/4 c. mayonnaise
1/4 c. plain yogurt
2 T. grated Vidalia onion
Juice of 1 lemon
1/2 c. celery, diced
1/2 c. pineapple, diced
Dash of thyme
Salt and pepper to taste
1/2 c. green grapes, halved
Lettuce of the season

Heat oil in non-stick pan, add chicken and weight chicken down with a heavy plate so it cooks evenly. Turn and remove when fully cooked, plump and firm. Refrigerate while you prepare the rest of the salad. Mix mayonnaise and yogurt. Add onion and lemon juice; refrigerate. Mix celery and pineapple. Cut chicken into bite size pieces. Toss all ingredients except grapes and lettuce. Line individual plates with lettuce leaves, add chicken salad and top with grapes.

Mexican Fiesta Delicioso!

M E ❧ N U

Nanci M. Newcomb, President
Delaware Federation of Garden Clubs

Margaritas	Mexican Beer	Fine Wines
Salsa Cruda*	Gazpacho Salsa*	Guacamole
Rio Grande Melon Salsa		Jalapeño Poppers*
Mexican Chicken Soup*		Rice with Crab*
Shrimp Veracruz		Chile Relenos

Salsa Cruda

3 tomatoes, cut and drained
1 Vidalia onion
1 green pepper, chopped
1 jalapeño pepper, chopped fine
3 T. cilantro, chopped
3 T. vinegar

Mix together and refrigerate.

Gazpacho Salsa

2 tomatillos, husked and rinsed
1 large ripe tomato
1/2 cucumber, peeled
1/2 large red bell pepper, seeded
1/2 large yellow bell pepper, seeded
1/4 medium red onion, peeled

1 serrano chile with seeds, minced
1 clove garlic, peeled and finely minced (optional)
2 T. fresh cilantro, minced
2 T. extra-virgin olive oil
2 T. sherry vinegar
1/4 t. salt

Cut the tomatillos, tomato, cucumber, bell peppers and onion into 1/2" pieces, dicing as neatly as possible. Combine with all other ingredients in a mixing bowl. Let sit at least 1 hour in refrigerator before using. Strain off some of the excess juice immediately before serving.

Jalapeño Poppers

24 large fat, firm jalapeño peppers
4 sun dried tomatoes in olive oil
1 pkg. feta cheese
8 oz. non-fat cream cheese
4-8 oz. Monterey jack cheese
2 chopped shallots
1/2 c. basil, parsley and thyme, chopped
1/4 c. cilantro, chopped
Garlic to taste

Slice jalapeño peppers in half lengthwise; save stem. Remove seeds. Add remaining ingredients together, mixing well. Fill peppers with cheese mixture. Freeze for 24 hours. Bake at 400 until cheese is melted.

Mexican Chicken Soup

1 4-1/2 to 5 pound stewing chicken, cut up
6 c. water
3-4 onion slices
3 stalks celery, cut up
1 t. salt
1/8 t. pepper
1 16 oz. can tomatoes, cut up
3 medium carrots, thinly sliced
1 medium onion, chopped
4 t. instant chicken bouillon granules
1 small zucchini, thinly sliced
1 c. frozen peas
1 small avocado, seeded, peeled and sliced

In Dutch oven combine chicken, water, onion, celery, salt and pepper. Simmer, covered, for 2 hours or until chicken is tender. Remove chicken from broth. Strain broth, discarding vegetables; return broth to Dutch oven. Add undrained tomatoes, sliced carrots, chopped onion and bouillon granules; simmer, covered, for 30 minutes or until the carrots are tender. Remove skin and bones from chicken; discard. Cube chicken; add to broth along with zucchini and peas. Cover and simmer 10-15 minutes longer or until vegetables are tender. Just before serving, garnish with avocado slices.

Rice with Crab

3/4 c. long grain rice
1 small onion, finely chopped
1 small clove garlic, minced
2 T. cooking oil
1-1/4 c. water
1 8 oz. can tomatoes, cut up
1-1/2 t. instant chicken bouillon granules
1/4 t. salt
Bottled hot pepper sauce
1/2 c. frozen peas
1 lb. fresh crabmeat or 1 7-1/2 oz. can, drained
2 T. dry sherry

In skillet cook rice, onion and garlic in oil over medium-low heat, stirring occasionally, until rice is golden brown. Remove from heat. Add water, undrained tomatoes, bouillon granules, salt and a few dashes hot pepper sauce. Cover and simmer about 15 minutes or until most of the liquid is absorbed. Stir in peas; cook 5 minutes more. Stir in crab and sherry; heat through.

Judge's Luncheon Menu

M E N U

Mrs. Alex H. Hilliard, President
Florida Federation of Garden Clubs, Inc.

Chicken Almond Bake*   Beans-in-a-Bundle*
Tomato Aspic*   or   Baked Apricots*
Frozen Chocolate Frango*

Chicken Almond Bake

6 c. chopped cooked chicken
1 large jar pimientos, chopped
4 T. onions, grated
2 cans mushroom soup
2 cans cream of celery soup
1 pkg. sliced almonds
3 c. milk
12 T. flour
3 small jars mushrooms and/or 3 cans sliced water chestnuts
48 slices bread, crusts removed
8 eggs, beaten
1/2 c. milk
2 or 3 large pkgs. potato chips, crushed

Mix flour and 3 cups milk until smooth. Cook, adding soups until thick. Add chicken, mushrooms, water chestnuts and onion; fold in pimientos. In 2 quart flat rectangular dish, make sandwiches, using six slices bread on bottom. Cover each with cooled mixture, top with six slices of bread. Use four rectangular dishes and repeat. Cover the dishes with plastic wrap and refrigerate overnight. Next day, cut each sandwich in half, dip in eggs which have been beaten with 1/2 cup of milk added. Roll in potato chip crumbs and place in buttered baking dish. Sprinkle sliced almonds over top. Bake at 350 for 30 minutes. This will make 48 half sandwiches. May be frozen before dipping in milk-egg mixture. Serves 30 to 36.

Beans-in-a-Bundle

4 pkgs. frozen whole green beans
1 lb. thin sliced bacon
2 2 oz. jars pimiento strips (optional)
2 8 oz. bottles Wishbone Sweet and Spicy French Dressing

Defrost beans by slightly cooking in large flat pan. Wrap 8 to 12 beans in one half slice of bacon. Place in pyrex dish, pour dressing over beans, and marinate overnight. Bake in same pan 25 minutes at 350 or until bacon is done. Garnish with pimiento strips, if desired. Serves 20-24.

Tomato Aspic

1 bunch celery hearts, finely chopped
1 medium onion, minced
4 heaping T. sweet relish
4 pkgs. lemon gelatin
4 cans tomato soup
Salt to taste

Mix celery, onion, sweet relish and dry gelatin. Heat soup with salt to boiling point. Do not add water. Pour over mixture. Stir until gelatin is dissolved. Pour into individual molds. Makes 24 1/3-cup servings.

Baked Apricots

Large cans apricots (unpeeled halves)
Butter
Brown Sugar
Ritz crackers, crushed

Drain apricot halves, reserving approximately 1/4 cup juice from each can. Place apricots, cut side up, in shallow buttered baking dish or pie pan. Dot each half with butter, sprinkle with brown sugar, and then sprinkle with crushed crackers. Drizzle with apricot juice. Bake in 350 oven approximately 25 to 30 minutes. Serve hot or cold.

Frozen Chocolate Frango

2 c. butter or margarine
4 c. sifted confectioner's sugar
8 1 oz. squares unsweetened chocolate, melted
8 eggs
1-1/2 t. peppermint flavoring
4 t. vanilla
2 c. chocolate wafer crumbs
Whipped cream for topping
Maraschino cherries, for topping

Using an electric mixer, beat together the butter and confectioner's sugar until light and fluffy. Add the melted chocolate and continue beating thoroughly. Add eggs, and beat again until fluffy. Then beat in peppermint and vanilla. Sprinkle about half of the cookie crumbs in 36 cupcake pan liners. Spoon the chocolate mixture into the liners, then top with the remaining crumbs. Freeze until firm. When ready to serve, top each with whipped cream and red or green cherries. Makes 36 small servings.

Favorite Recipes

M E ❧ N U

Helen Jordan, President
The Garden Club of Georgia, Inc.

Baked Fish with Cheese & Potato Chips   Deviled Crab*
Cold Rice Salad   Favorite Chicken Breasts*
Grapefruit Salad *   Marinated Vidalia Onions
Pineapple Chiffon Pie   Butterscotch Pie*

Deviled Crab

1 lb. crabmeat
1 c. evaporated milk
1/2 c. chopped green peppers
1 t. hot sauce
1 c. Miracle Whip
1/2 c. chopped celery
1/4 c. chopped onion
1 t. Worcestershire sauce
Approximately 1-1/2 c. saltine crackers, coarsely crushed
with hands

Mix all ingredients thoroughly, adding enough crackers to give good consistency. Put in individual crab shells or bake in a casserole. Dot with butter and sprinkle with finely crushed cracker crumbs. Bake 30 minutes for shells and about 1 hour for a casserole in a 350 oven.

Favorite Chicken Breasts

8 chicken breasts (halves, skinned and boned)
8 slices bacon
1 4 oz. package chipped beef
1 can cream of mushroom soup
1 c. sour cream

Arrange chipped beef in 9x13" casserole. Roll chicken breasts, wrap with bacon, secure with toothpick. Place on beef. Mix sour cream with soup. Spread over chicken. Cover and refrigerate. Bake uncovered in 275 degree oven for 2-1/2 to 3 hours depending on size of breasts. Serves 8.

Grapefruit Salad

2 envelopes gelatin combined with 4 T. water
2/3 c. boiling water
2/3 c. sugar
2 c. grapefruit sections and juice (3 large or 4 small)

Add the boiling water to the softened gelatin. Stir well and add the sugar. Stir well again and add to grapefruit and juice. Pour into oblong or square glass casserole. Refrigerate and congeal then spread with cream cheese, softened with milk, and sprinkle with chopped nuts.

Butterscotch Pie

1 9-inch pie shell, baked
2 eggs, separated
1 c. brown sugar
1/8 t. salt
4 T. cake flour
1-1/2 c. milk
4 T. butter
1 t. vanilla extract
4 T. granulated sugar

Combine beaten egg yolks, brown sugar, salt, flour, milk and butter in a double boiler. Cook over boiling water, stirring constantly until it thickens. Then cover and cook 15 minutes stirring occasionally. Cool, add vanilla and pour into baked pie shell. Cover with meringue made from the two egg whites and the 4 T. granulated sugar. Bake at 350 degrees until brown.

Family Favorites

M E ❧ N U

Sandra Ford, President
Idaho Garden Clubs, Inc.

Soybean Minestrone* Potato-Leek Soup*
Mexican Salad* Leg of Lamb with Lemon Garlic Sauce*
Saffron Rice* Asparagus Menestra*
Basque Custard Flan* Cardamom Finnish Coffee Bread*

Soybean Minestrone

3 T. olive oil
1/2 c. brown rice
1 large onion, chopped
1/4 lb. mushrooms, halved
1 c. carrots, thickly sliced
1/2 c. green pepper, chopped
1/2 c. celery, chopped
2-1/2 c. cooked soybeans or 2 15oz. cans, rinsed and drained
1 28 oz. can tomatoes, including liquid
5 c. water
7 vegetable or beef-flavored bouillon cubes
1 t. rosemary
1 t. oregano leaves
1 t. dry basil
1/2 t. thyme leaves
1/2 t. summer savory
1/4 t. cayenne
1 c. elbow macaroni

1 c. dry red wine
1 c. zucchini, thickly sliced
1/2 c. parsley, chopped
Grated Parmesan cheese

Heat oil in a 4 or 5 quart Dutch oven over medium-high heat; add rice, onion and mushrooms. Cook, stirring frequently, until golden. Add carrots, green pepper, celery, and tomatoes. Stir to break up tomatoes. Add soybeans, water, bouillon cubes, spices and macaroni. Stir in 1/2 cup of the red wine. Bring mixture to a boil, then decrease heat and simmer for 40 minutes, stirring occasionally. Add zucchini and cook about 8 minutes or until zucchini is tender to bite. Stir in remaining 1/2 cup of wine and sprinkle with parsley. Pass Parmesan cheese to add to individual servings.

Potato-Leek Soup

4 T. butter
1/2 small onion
9 leeks, cut, split ends
6-7 large potatoes, cut in 1" long slices
2 t. salt
1 carrot, cut in 1/2" slices
1 cube chicken bouillon

Refrito ingredients (optional)
4 T. olive oil
1-1/2 cloves garlic, chopped
Pinch crushed red pepper flakes
1 T. red wine vinegar

In a large pot, melt butter, add chicken bouillon, salt and onions; sauté for 10 minutes. Add chopped leeks and carrots; sauté for 5 minutes; add potatoes. Cook for 30 minutes on medium high, until potatoes are tender. To make the refrito, in a saucepan sauté oil, garlic and crushed red pepper until garlic turns light color. Add vinegar and pour over soup. Let boil for 5-10 minutes.

Mexican Salad

1-1/2 lb. lean hamburger
1 onion, chopped
1 15 oz. can dark kidney beans, drained
Salt and pepper to taste
1/2 t. chili powder
1/4 t. cayenne pepper
1 T. Italian herb seasoning
1 head lettuce, shredded
2 tomatoes, divided
1-1/2 c. grated sharp cheese
1 c. celery, chopped
1 4-1/2 oz. can chopped or sliced black olives
1 bag nacho chips
1/2-1 c. mayonnaise
2 T. relish
2 T. catsup or thousand island dressing
1 avocado

Cook hamburger and onion in a large skillet. Drain. Add kidney beans and seasonings. Mix well and remove from heat to cool. In a large bowl mix lettuce, one diced tomato, cheese, celery, olives and 2 handfuls of crushed nachos. Blend mayonnaise, relish and catsup or dressing in a separate bowl. Add to lettuce and mix well. Add cooled hamburger and mix. Arrange wedges of tomato and avocado in a circle on top of salad. Stand whole nacho chips around edge of bowl.

Leg of Lamb with Lemon-Garlic Sauce

3 lb. leg of lamb
1/2 c. Spanish olive oil
1/2 c. freshly squeezed lemon juice
4-6 cloves garlic, minced
Freshly ground pepper
Salt

Place lamb in shallow glass baking dish. Slowly whisk oil into lemon juice. Pour over meat. Sprinkle with garlic and generous amount of pepper. Chill 24 hours, turning occasionally. Bring lamb to room temperature. Preheat oven to 325. Place meat and marinade in shallow roasting pan. Sprinkle with salt. Roast 2 to 3 hours, depending on desired doneness, basting frequently with pan juices. Slice and serve with pan juices.

Saffron Rice

2 T. Spanish olive oil
1/4 c. finely chopped onion
1-1/2 c. uncooked long grain white rice
3 c. boiling water
1/2 t. salt
1/4 t. pulverized saffron threads

Heat oil in a heavy 12" skillet until light haze forms. Add onions and cook until soft and transparent. Add rice and stir to coat with oil. Add water, salt and saffron. Bring to a boil, stirring, then cover skillet tightly and reduce heat to lowest point. Simmer 20 minutes or until liquid has been absorbed.

Asparagus Menestra

2 lb. asparagus tips
2 T. Spanish olive oil
1/2 c. chopped onion
2 oz. chorizo, cut into thin rounds
1/4 c. diced salt pork
1-1/2 T. flour
1 c. dry white wine
1/2 c. liquid from asparagus

Steam asparagus tips until tender, but not over-cooked. Reserve 1/2 cup liquid from steaming. Heat oil in heavy skillet over moderate heat until light haze forms. Add onion, chorizo and salt pork. When onion is translucent, add flour and stir gently. Add wine and asparagus liquid.   Bring to a boil, then pour over asparagus.

Basque Custard Flan

1/3 c. sugar
6 eggs
4 c. milk
1 c. sugar
1 t. vanilla
1 t. nutmeg
Pinch of salt

On top of stove, brown the 1/3 cup of sugar in a 3" deep and 5 cup capacity baking pan, set aside. Beat the eggs, add milk. Stir in sugar, vanilla, nutmeg and salt; mix well. Pour into the prepared baking pan. Set this in a pan of warm water and place in 325 oven and bake for 1 hour.

Cardamom Finnish Coffee Bread

1/2 c. warm water, 110-115
2 pkgs. active dry yeast
1 c. milk
4 eggs
1 c. sugar
10 whole cardamom pods, cracked open and seeds pounded
7 to 7-1/2 c. sifted flour, divided
1/2 c. soft margarine or butter
2 t. salt
1 egg beaten
1/2 c. sliced almonds
Coarse sugar

Dissolve yeast in warm water. Heat milk until lukewarm; add dissolved yeast and stir. In a large warm mixing bowl, beat eggs and sugar until foamy. Add milk, cardamom and 2 cups flour. Beat at medium speed for 2 minutes until smooth and elastic. Stir in softened butter, salt and enough flour to make dough stiff enough to knead. Knead on floured surface until smooth and satiny, about 5 to 10 minutes. Place in a greased warm bowl, turning to grease top. Cover, let rise in warm place until light and doubled in size. On floured surface divide dough into three parts. Divide each third into three parts. Form each part in a strip 16" long. Braid three together, sealing ends. Repeat for remaining two loaves. Place on greased cookie sheets. Cover loosely and let rise about 30 minutes until less than doubled in size. Brush loaves with egg; sprinkle with almonds and sugar. Bake at 375 for 20-25 minutes.

Duck Dinner Welsh Style

M E N U

Miriam H. Davies, President
The Garden Club of Illinois, Inc.

Stuffed Grapefruit*
Roast Duck* with Sage & Onion Stuffing*

Roast Potatoes	Giblet Gravy
Rutabaga Sprouts	Apple Sauce

Raspberry Flan with Whipped Cream

Stuffed Grapefruit

Grapefruit
Kiwi fruit
Cooked cranberries
Mint leaves
Fresh strawberries

Wash the grapefruit and cut in half by making criss-cross cuts. Remove the flesh and clean off skin. Set shells aside. Cut flesh into small pieces and place in a bowl. Add fresh Kiwi fruit and cooked cranberries to fill the empty grapefruit shells. Serve garnished with mint and a strawberry.

Roast Duck

Clean duck; remove fat and giblets. Use giblets to make gravy.
Stuff the duck and place in shallow open pan. Cook slowly at 300.

Sage & Onion Stuffing
3 onions, chopped finely
2 eggs
1/2 stick margarine, melted and cooled
6 slices stale bread
2 t. powdered sage

Sauté onions until softened; drain on paper towels. In large bowl,
slightly beat eggs. Add all the ingredients and stuff the duck.

Good Ole Dressing

24 slices bread, broken
48 saltine crackers, broken
1 c. chopped turkey
6 boiled eggs, chopped
1 small onion, chopped
1/2 cup chopped parsley
Hot broth, enough to moisten

Mix ingredients; put in 9x13" pan. Bake at 425 until done.

Candied Sweet Potatoes

4 medium sweet potatoes
1/4 c. butter
1 egg
2 t. salt
1 t. nutmeg
2 t. brown sugar
2 t. butter
Small marshmallows

Boil and mash sweet potatoes; combine with butter, egg, salt and nutmeg. Beat until creamy. Spoon into 8" baking dish. Sprinkle with brown sugar and dot with butter. Top with marshmallows and bake, uncovered, at 350 for 30 minutes or until marshmallows are brown. Serves 6-8.

Frozen Cranberry Salad

2 envelopes Dream Whip
12 oz. cream cheese
4 T. mayonnaise
4 T. sugar
2 15 oz. cans cranberry sauce
2 c. crushed pineapple, drained
2 c. nuts, chopped

Prepare Dream Whip; refrigerate. Whip cream cheese, mayonnaise and sugar. Add cranberry sauce, pineapple and nuts. Fold in Dream Whip. Pour into 10x13" pyrex dish. Freeze. Serve on lettuce. Serves 18-24.

Corn Casserole

2 T. butter
1/2 c. onion, diced
1/4 c. green pepper, chopped
2 cans whole kernel corn, drained
1 c. sour cream
3-4 bacon slices, cooked, drained and crumbled

Sauté onion and green pepper in butter in large skillet. Add sour cream and drained corn. Heat through and serve. Top serving dish with bacon. Serves 8-10.

Mamo Parker's Pumpkin Pie

1-1/2 c. sugar
1 T. flour
1 t. cinnamon
1/8 t. nutmeg
1/8 t. ginger
2 eggs
2 c. pumpkin
2 c. sweet milk
Unbaked pie crust

Put ingredients together in order given. Put mixture into unbaked pie crust. Bake as for custard pie. This makes 2 small pies. For 9" or larger pie, make 1-1/2 times the recipe for 2 pies.

Dutch Apple Pie

4-6 apples
1/2 c. sugar
1 t. cinnamon
3/4 c. flour
1/3 c. butter or margarine
1/2 c. brown sugar

Mix apples, sugar and cinnamon; put into unbaked crust. Mix flour, butter or margarine and sugar. Spread over apples. Bake at 375 until done, about 1 hour.

Deviled Clams

6 large clams 3-4" across
1/4 c. butter
1 clove garlic, minced
1/2 c. onion, chopped
1/3 c. green bell pepper, chopped
1/3 c. celery, chopped
1/2 c. cracker crumbs
1/2 c. bread crumbs
2 T. parsley, chopped
1/2 t. salt
1/4 t. black pepper
1/8 t. cayenne pepper
6 drops Tabasco sauce
2 t. prepared mustard
1/2 t. thyme
1 egg, beaten

Scrub and shuck clams; save shells. Drain and chop clams; save liquid. Melt butter in skillet. Sauté garlic, onion, pepper and celery until onion is transparent. Add clams with liquid and simmer over low heat 5 minutes. Remove from heat; add remaining ingredients and mix together. Fill 6 shells. Flavor is best if baked on a bed of rock salt. Bake at 350 for 30 minutes.

Milly Way's Cream of Zucchini Soup

4 medium zucchini, sliced and quartered
2 cans chicken broth
1 bunch green onions, chopped
1 t. salt
1 t. pepper
Dill weed to taste
2 8 oz. pkgs. cream cheese
1 c. sour cream

To chicken broth in saucepan, add zucchini, green onions, salt, pepper and dill weed. Cook 20-30 minutes until vegetables are tender. Cool. In blender, mix cheese and sour cream until smooth. Blend in zucchini mixture in small portions. Chill thoroughly.

Raspberry-Plum Sorbet

2 c. frozen raspberries, thawed
3 small-medium purple plums
1/2 c. sugar
1/3 c. water
1 T. light corn syrup

Combine sugar water and syrup. Heat, stirring to dissolve sugar. Bring to boil and remove from heat. Put raspberries in blender with juice and blend until smooth. Strain to remove seeds. Return to blender; add chopped plums. Blend well, but not completely smooth. The flecks of purple skin add interest. Add syrup mixture and blend. Freeze in ice cream maker or pour into mold, freeze in refrigerator freezer. When partially frozen, remove and beat thoroughly. Repeat partial freezing and beating one more time.

Venison

6 center cut steaks
3 T. freshly ground black pepper
Kosher salt
3 T. corn oil
3 T. minced shallots
1 c. Pinot Noir
3/4 c. chicken stock
1/3 c. dried bing cherries, soaked in warm water until plump
2 T. Italian parsley, chopped
6 T. unsalted butter

Wipe steaks with damp paper towel. Sprinkle generously with pepper and lightly with salt. With mallet or saucer, pound pepper into steaks. Heat oil and brown steaks on both sides. Remove from pan and place in warm oven. Pour excess oil away. Sauté shallots, scraping pan. Add wine, chicken stock, cherries and parsley. Boil until liquid is reduced by half. Add butter and juices from steak platter. Boil to thicken. Return steaks to pan. Simmer and baste 1 minute or so. Serve immediately.

Carrot Soufflé

1 lb. carrots, peeled and sliced
Salt to taste
1/2 c. melted butter or margarine
1/2 c. sugar
1 t. baking powder
3 T. flour
3 eggs
1 t. vanilla extract

Cook carrots in salted water until tender; drain. Combine with butter in blender or food processor until smooth. Combine sugar, baking powder, flour, eggs and vanilla in a bowl; mix well. Add the carrot mixture; mix well. Spoon into greased baking dish. Bake at 350 for 45 minutes.

Broccoli

1 medium head broccoli
2 T. butter or margarine
1/8 t. salt
2 t. lemon juice
2 T. bread crumbs
1 hard cooked egg

Ahead of time, melt butter; add salt, lemon juice and bread crumbs. Brown slightly. Force hard cooked egg through sieve and keep refrigerated until ready to serve. When ready to prepare, cook broccoli head until just tender, about 10-15 minutes. Sprinkle flower tops with hard cooked egg and then bread crumbs. Serve immediately.

Jasmine Rice

3 cups water
1 cup Jasmine rice, purchased
at store carrying international foods

Bring water and rice to boil; simmer 20 minutes. Let stand until water is absorbed.

Spinach Salad with Apple-Onion Vinaigrette

1 bag spinach
1/2 c. sugar
1/2 c. apple cider vinegar
1 t. grated purple onion
1/2 t. dry mustard
1/2 t. salt
1/4 c. vegetable oil
3/4 c. chopped apple

Wash and dry spinach. Thoroughly mix remaining ingredients. Put dressing on spinach at serving time.

White Chocolate Mousse with Frangelico

8 oz. best quality white chocolate, broken into small pieces
1/2 c. unsalted butter
6 eggs, separated, room temperature
1 c. sifted confectioner's sugar
1/2 c. Frangelico liqueur
2 c. whipping cream, cold
Pinch cream of tartar
Unsweetened powdered cocoa or shaved chocolate

Melt white chocolate and butter in small saucepan, stirring constantly. Set aside. Beat the egg yolks, sugar and liqueur until the mixture forms a slowly dissolving ribbon when the beaters are lifted. Pour the mixture into the top of a double boiler and cook, whisking constantly, over simmering water until very thick, about 3 minutes. Remove to a large mixing bowl. Whisk in the white chocolate mixture and stir until smooth; cool. Beat the cream until the peaks are stiff. In a separate bowl, with clean beaters, beat the egg whites with the cream of tartar until stiff but not dry. Gently fold the egg whites into the chocolate mixture; then fold in the whipped cream. Refrigerate, covered, until set, at least 3 hours. Spoon into individual serving dishes and sprinkle with cocoa or chocolate.

Crawfish Jambalaya in Hitachi

1-1/2 c. raw rice, using Hitachi measuring cup
1 can beef broth
1 c. onion, chopped
1 c. bell pepper, chopped
1 jalapeño pepper, chopped
1 stick margarine or butter, melted
1 8 oz. can tomato sauce
1 4 oz. can mushrooms, drained and chopped
1 lb. crawfish tails, chopped if large

Wash rice and drain. Place all ingredients in 8-10 cup rice cooker with drained rice. Do not add any water. Taste for seasoning. Add salt and pepper, if needed. Put rice cooker on cook cycle. After cook cycle is completed, keep on warm cycle for at least 1/2 hour. Precooked chopped beef, pork or chicken may be used in place of crawfish tails, if desired, using an additional 1/2 cup of broth or water.

Seafood Enchiladas

1 lb. crawfish tails, shrimp or drained crabmeat
1 can cream of shrimp soup
1 8 oz. carton sour cream
1/2 c. chopped green chilies
1 c. onion, chopped fine
8 oz. mild cheddar cheese, grated
8 oz. Monterey Jack cheese, grated
1 pkg. 8-10 flour tortillas

Heat soup, sour cream, green chilies, onions and 1/2 of the grated cheese until the cheese melts. Add about 1/3 of the sauce to coat the seafood you are using. Place mixture on tortilla and sprinkle with a little grated cheese; then roll up. Place in a casserole dish which has a little sauce on the bottom; cover with remaining sauce and the rest of the grated cheese. Bake at 325 for 15-20 minutes or until bubbly and all the cheese is melted.

Chicken Jambalaya

1 3-4 lb. fryer, cut in serving pieces
1/2 c. olive oil
2 c. onion, finely chopped
6 shallots, chopped
2 cloves garlic, mashed
1 c. green bell pepper, chopped
1/4 t. red pepper
2 T. salt
1 bay leaf
1 14-1/2 oz. can tomatoes
Tabasco and Worcestershire sauces to taste
2-1/2 c. rice
5 c. water
1/2 c. sherry wine
1 4 oz. can mushrooms
1 14-1/2 oz. can English peas

Brown chicken in olive oil over medium heat. Remove chicken and sauté onions, shallots, garlic and green pepper in same oil; adding more oil if needed. Cook until lightly brown. Add pepper, salt, bay leaf, tomatoes and sauces. Cook slowly for 6-7 minutes. Add browned chicken, rice, water and wine; turn to high. Bring to boiling point. Add mushrooms and peas; remove from fire. Cover saucepan and place in oven, preheated to 400, cook for about 45 minutes.

Louisiana Traditional Hot Meat Pies

Filling:
1 T. shortening
2 T. flour
1/2 lb. ground beef
1-1/2 lb. ground pork
2 c. onions, chopped
1 c. green onions, chopped
3 T. fresh parsley, chopped
Salt, red pepper, garlic powder to taste

Make a roux of shortening and flour. Add other ingredients. Cook thoroughly; let cool before making pies.

Pastry:
4 c. flour
2 t. baking powder
1/2 c. shortening, not vegetable oil
2 eggs, beaten
Milk

Sift flour and baking powder together twice. Put in bowl and add shortening and eggs. Add enough milk to make a stiff dough. Roll out very thin. Use a saucer to cut circle of dough. Fill one side of circle with filling and fold over. Dampen edge with water and crimp with a fork. Fry in deep hot fat until golden brown. Drain well. Serve hot. Pies can be baked instead of fried by placing on greased baking sheet and baking at 350 for 20 minutes or until golden brown. Makes 18 pies.

Cajun Crawfish Cornbread

2 c. corn meal
1 t. salt
1 t. baking soda
1 c. onions, chopped
3/4 c. celery, chopped
1/4 c. jalapeño pepper, chopped
16 oz. cheddar cheese, grated
1/2 c. oil
6 eggs, beaten
2 16 oz. cans cream style corn
2 lb. crawfish, chopped or 1 lb. crawfish and 1 lb. crabmeat

Mix all ingredients together until thoroughly blended. Bake in a well greased 12x14" pan at 375 for 45-50 minutes or until golden brown. Will serve 15-20 and freezes well.

Luncheon

M E N U

Mrs. Edward J. Hinman, President
The Federated Garden Clubs of Maryland, Inc.

Crab Cakes*   Broiled Tomatoes*
French Bread   Fruit Cobbler*

Crab Cakes

1 lb. lump crabmeat
1 T. Old Bay seafood seasoning
2 t. fresh parsley, chopped
1 egg, lightly beaten
1 T. mayonnaise
3 T. dry fresh bread crumbs

Remove all cartilage from crabmeat, mix lightly with other ingredients. Make into uniform cakes. Fry in butter or spray pan with non-stick cooking spray. Brown on both sides, serve while hot. Serves 6.

Broiled Tomatoes

1/3 c. dry bread crumbs
3 T. Italian dressing
1 T. fresh parsley, chopped
3 medium size tomatoes, halved
Dash of salt and pepper

Combine bread crumbs, dressing and parsley in a small bowl; mix well.   Spoon bread crumb mixture over cut surface of tomato, sprinkle with salt and pepper. Broil about 4-5" from heat, about 7 minutes or until topping is lightly browned. Serves 6.

Fruit Cobbler

1/2 c. butter or margarine
1 c. sugar
1 c. flour
1 t. baking powder
1/2 t. salt
2/3 c. milk
1 c. fresh fruit

Melt butter or margarine in 9x12" baking dish. Sift together sugar, flour, baking powder and salt; stir in milk. Pour over melted butter in pan. Top with fruit of choice. Bake 1 hour at 350.

Minnesota Chicken Dinner

M E N U

Violet Hague, President
Federated Garden Clubs of Minnesota, Inc.

Cranberry Chicken*   Wild Rice Casserole*
Mandarin Salad* with Sweet-Sour Dressing*
Lowell Inn Crescent Rolls*

Cranberry Chicken

1 8 oz. bottle French dressing
1 8 oz. can crushed pineapple
1 16 oz. can whole cranberries
1 t. dry mustard
1 1 oz. pkg. onion soup mix
8 skinned chicken breasts

Mix dressing, pineapple, cranberries, mustard and onion soup mix together.   Place chicken in 9x12" baking dish. Cover with sauce. Bake at 350 for 1 hour. Do not cover pan.

Wild Rice Casserole

1 bunch green onions, chopped
8 oz. fresh mushrooms
1 stick margarine
2 cans consommé
1/2 c. chopped celery
1 c. wild rice, washed

Sauté onions and mushrooms in margarine. Add consommé and celery; mix together in casserole with rice. Bake, uncovered, 1-1/4 hours in 350 oven. Do not stir. Add a little water during baking, if too dry.

Mandarin Salad

1/4 c. sliced almonds
1 T. and 1 t. sugar
1/4 head of lettuce, torn in pieces
1/4 bunch romaine, torn in pieces
1 c. chopped celery
2 green onions, chopped
1 11 oz. can mandarin oranges

Cook almonds and sugar over low heat, stirring constantly until sugar is melted and almonds are coated. Place lettuce, romaine, celery and onions in bowl. Add sweet-sour dressing and oranges. Toss until coated and then add almonds.

Sweet-Sour Dressing

1/4 c. oil
2 T. sugar
1/2 t. salt
2 T. vinegar
1 T. parsley, chopped
Dash of pepper

Shake all ingredients in covered jar. Refrigerate.

Lowell Inn Crescent Rolls

3/4 c. lukewarm water
2 pkgs. active yeast
1/2 c. sugar
1 t. salt
2 eggs
4 c. flour, divided
Melted butter

In a large bowl, dissolve yeast in lukewarm water. Stir in the sugar, salt, eggs and 2 cups of flour. Add 2 more cups flour and mix until smooth. Scrape dough from sides of bowl, cover with a damp cloth. Let rise until double, about 1-1/2 hours. Punch dough down, divide into two parts. Roll 1/2 of dough into circle. Cut circle into 16 wedges and roll up. Place on greased cookie sheet. Repeat with other 1/2 of dough. Brush with butter, cover and let rise until double, about 1 hour. Bake at 400 for 12-15 minutes. Makes 32 rolls.

24 Hour Wine and Cheese Omelet

1 large loaf day-old French or Italian bread,
broken into small pieces
6 T. unsalted butter, melted
3/4 lb. Domestic Swiss cheese, shredded
1/2 lb. Monterey Jack cheese, shredded
9 thin slices Genoa salami, coarsely chopped
16 eggs
3-1/4 c. milk
1/2 c. dry white wine
4 large whole green onions, minced
1 T. German mustard
1/4 t. freshly ground pepper
1/8 t. ground red pepper
1-1/2 c. sour cream
2/3-1 cup fresh grated Parmesan or shredded Asiago cheese

Butter 2 shallow 9x13" baking dishes. Spread bread over bottom
and drizzle with butter. Sprinkle with Swiss and Jack cheeses and

salami. Beat together eggs, milk, wine, green onions, mustard, pepper and red pepper until foamy. Pour over cheese. Cover dishes with foil, crimping edges. Refrigerate overnight. Remove from refrigerator about 30 minutes before baking. Preheat oven to 325. Bake casseroles, covered, until set, about 1 hour. Uncover; spread with sour cream and sprinkle with remaining cheese. Bake uncovered until crusty and lightly browned, about 10 minutes. Makes 12 servings.

Sugared Bacon

1 lb. bacon, room temperature, not thick sliced
1-1/4 c. brown sugar
1 T. cinnamon (optional)

Cut each slice of bacon in half, crosswise. Mix sugar and cinnamon together and thoroughly coat each slice of bacon. Twist slices, or leave flat, and place on rack in a broiler or jellyroll pan in a 350 oven. Bake until bacon is crisp and sugar is bubbly, 15-20 minutes. Watch closely as the sugar burns quickly. Cool on foil. Serve at room temperature. These may be made hours ahead and left at room temperature. Makes 16 servings.

Family Brunch Cake

2/3 c. brown sugar, packed
2/3 c. sifted cake flour
1 t. cinnamon
4 T. butter
1/2 c. butter
1 8 oz. pkg. cream cheese
1-1/4 c. sugar
2 eggs
1 t. vanilla
2 c. sifted cake flour
1 t. baking powder
1/2 t. soda
1/4 t. salt
1/4 c. milk

Combine first 4 ingredients and mix until crumbly. Cream the 1/2 cup butter, cream cheese and sugar. Add eggs and vanilla and beat well. Sift together the dry ingredients and add alternately with milk to creamed mixture, mixing well after each addition. Pour into a greased and floured 9x13" pan. Sprinkle with the crumb mixture. Bake in 350 oven 35-40 minutes.

Dining in the Desert, Vegas Style

M E ❧ N U

Mrs. William F. Pearns, President
Nevada Garden Clubs, Inc.

Highroller Dip*   A Summer Delight Soup*
Gamblers Delight Salad*   Shrimp Scampi*
Asparagus with Hollandaise Sauce   Rice Pilaf
Lee's Jackpot*

Highroller Dip

2 3 oz. pkgs. cream cheese
2 t. lemon juice
2 t. grated onion or 3 drops onion juice
1 t. Worcestershire sauce
3-4 drops Tabasco sauce
1/4 t. salt
1 7 or 7-1/2 oz. can minced clams, chilled and drained
1 T. minced parsley

Stir cream cheese to soften. Add lemon juice, onion, Worcestershire sauce, Tabaso sauce and salt. Beat with electric or rotary beater or electric blender until light and fluffy. Stir in clams and parsley. Trim with parsley. Serve with chips, crackers and crisp vegetables. Makes about 1-1/2 cups.

A Summer Delight Soup

1 c. pureed avocado
1 c. sour cream
1 c. canned jellied chicken consommé
1 t. lime juice
Grated orange peel

Mix all ingredients. Chill and serve in cold cups. Garnish with watercress leaves.

Gamblers Delight Salad (No Cherries)

10 large cooked shrimp, shelled and deveined
1/4 cantaloupe, peeled and cut in wedges
6 green grapes, halved
Mayonnaise flavored with curry to taste
Lettuce leaves

Place cantaloupe wedge on bed of lettuce. Arrange shrimp on top of wedge.   Cover with curried mayonnaise.   Garnish with grapes. Serves one.

Shrimp Scampi

12 oz. fresh or frozen shrimp, peeled and deveined
2 T. margarine or butter
3 cloves garlic, minced
2 T. parsley, snipped
1 T. dry sherry

Thaw shrimp, if frozen. In a large skillet heat margarine or butter over medium high heat. Add shrimp and garlic. Cook, stirring frequently, for 1 to 3 minutes or until shrimp turn pink. Stir in parsley and sherry. Makes 4 servings.

Lee's Jackpot

1/2 stick butter
6 heaping T. brown sugar
4 bananas
1 T. banana liqueur, overflow a bit
1 T. light rum
2 T. brandy
Vanilla ice cream

Mix butter and brown sugar in skillet. Cook over medium heat until sugar is melted. Slice bananas in halves or quarters and add to butter mixture, cooking until tender. Add liqueur and stir. Sprinkle rum and brandy over top. Ignite. Spoon gently a few times. Serve warm over vanilla ice cream. Serves 6.

Buffet for a Special Occasion

M E N U

Jane Bersch, President
The Garden Club of New Jersey

Virginia Dip*   Sausage-Spinach Balls*
Currant Glazed Ham*   Crab-Shrimp Casserole*
Broccoli with Capers   Tomato Aspic
Country Potatoes   Angel Biscuits
Lemon Sponge Dessert* Tides Lodge Chocolate Chess Pie*
Spicy Fruit Bowl

Virginia Dip

1/2 c. pecans, chopped
2 t. butter
8 oz. cream cheese, softened
1 T. milk
1/4 c. green pepper, diced
1 pkg. dried beef
1/2 t. garlic powder
1 c. sour cream
4 t. onion, minced
1 t. horseradish

Sauté pecans in butter. Reserve. Mix rest of the ingredients thoroughly. Place in 1-1/2 quart baking dish, top with pecans. Chill until serving time. Bake at 350 for 20 minutes, until bubbly. Serve hot with crackers. Serves 10. Recipe may be doubled.

Sausage Spinach Balls

2 pkgs. frozen spinach, cooked, drained well
2 c. seasoned stuffing
1 c. grated Parmesan cheese
2 T. minced onion
6 eggs, well beaten
1/2-3/4 c. butter, melted
2 small cloves garlic, minced
1/2 t. pepper
4 oz. bulk sausage, cooked and drained

Preheat oven to 350. Combine all ingredients, mixing thoroughly. Form into small balls about the size of walnuts. Place on ungreased cookie sheet and bake at 350 for 20 minutes or until browned. Serve immediately. May be prepared ahead and flash frozen on cookie sheet. Thaw before baking.

Currant Glazed Ham

1 10 oz. jar red currant jelly
1/4 c. dry sherry
1 6-7 lb. fully cooked boneless ham

Combine currant jelly and sherry in small saucepan; cook over low heat, stirring constantly, until jelly melts. Remove from heat and set aside. Place ham, fat side up, on rack in a shallow roasting pan. Cover with foil. Bake at 325 for 1 hour. Remove foil and baste generously with jelly mixture. Bake uncovered, about 30 minutes or until a meat thermometer registers 140, basting every 15 minutes. Serves 12 to 14.

Crab-Shrimp Casserole

2-1/2 c. cooked rice
1 lb. crabmeat
1 lb. cooked shrimp
10 hard cooked eggs, chopped
3 c. mayonnaise
1/4 t. dried tarragon leaves
2 T. parsley
2 t. grated onion
2 6 oz. cans evaporated milk
1 t. salt
1 t. cayenne pepper
2 c. shredded sharp cheese
1 jar chopped pimiento

Mix all of the ingredients together and place in a 3 quart oblong casserole. Bake at 350 for 30 minutes. May be prepared a day ahead and stored in refrigerator. Will take a longer time to warm up. Serves about 16 people.

Lemon Sponge Dessert

2 T. butter, softened
2 c. sugar
4 T. flour
1/8 t. salt
5 T. lemon juice
Rind of 1 lemon, grated
3 eggs, separated
1-1/2 c. milk

Preheat oven to 325. Cream butter; add sugar, flour, salt, lemon juice and rind. Beat egg yolks, stir in milk and add to lemon mixture. Fold into stiffly beaten egg whites. Turn into a 2 quart baking dish set in a pan of water; bake 45 minutes or until inserted knife comes out clean. Refrigerate before serving. Serves 8.

Tides Lodge Chocolate Chess Pie

4 heaping T. cocoa
1-1/2 c. sugar
2 eggs, beaten
1/2 c. pecans, chopped
1/4 c. butter, melted
1/2 c. unsweetened evaporated milk
1/2 c. coconut
1 9" pie shell, unbaked
Vanilla ice cream

Preheat oven to 400. Mix all ingredients and pour into an unbaked pie shell. Bake for 30 minutes. Cool. Serve with a scoop of vanilla ice cream.

New Mexico Traditional Menu

M E ❧ N U

Elane McIlroy, President
New Mexico Garden Clubs, Inc.

Frozen Margaritas*   Sangria
Chile Con Queso with Tortilla Chips   Tortilla Soup*
Guacamole Salad*   Beef Tacos
Sour Cream Green Enchiladas*   Frijoles
Bizcochitos* (Official Cookie of New Mexico)

Frozen Margaritas

1 small can frozen limeade
1 can Tequila
3 t. Triple Sec
Ice
Lime (optional)
Salt (optional)

Fill 1 quart blender with mixture and ice. Can add some water so it will not be too icy. Blend. Coat glasses with lime and dip in salt, if desired.

Tortilla Soup

1 medium onion, chopped
2 cloves garlic, chopped
2 T. vegetable or olive oil
2 cans beef bouillon
2 cans chicken broth or homemade meat stock
1 can Rotel tomatoes and green chilies
1 can tomatoes
1 t. ground cumin
1 t. chili powder
1 t. salt
3/4 t. Worcestershire sauce
1 c. cooked, chicken, diced
1 large tomato, peeled and diced
Tortilla strips, fried crisp
Avocado slices
Monterey Jack cheese, grated

Sauté onion and garlic in oil. Add beef and chicken broths, tomatoes and spices. Bring to a boil, cover and simmer one hour. Add chicken and tomato. Cook 5 minutes. Cut tortillas into narrow strips and fry crisp. Place a few in bowls. Fill with the hot soup. Garnish with more tortilla strips, avocado slices and cheese.

Guacamole Salad

3 large avocados, peeled, seeded and mashed with fork
1 large tomato, chopped
1 medium onion, chopped
2-3 t. lemon juice
1/2 t. garlic salt
Green salsa to taste

Mix all the ingredients together and serve on a lettuce leaf.

Sour Cream Green Enchiladas

1 dozen corn tortillas
2 c. shredded Monterey Jack cheese
3/4 c. onion, chopped
1/4 c. margarine
1/4 c. flour
2 c. chicken broth
1 c. sour cream
1 4 oz. can chopped jalapeño peppers or jalapeño relish
1 c. cheddar cheese

Cook tortillas in oil 3 or 4 seconds on each side. Do not want to turn crisp. Place 2 tablespoons cheese and 1 tablespoon onion on each tortilla. Roll up and place seam side down in 9x13" baking dish. In a saucepan, melt margarine; blend in flour. Add chicken broth. Cook stirring constantly, until it thickens and bubbles. Add cream and peppers. Pour over enchiladas. Cook at 400 for 25 minutes. Sprinkle cheddar cheese over top. Return to oven until cheese is well melted. Serves 6 - 8.

Bizcochitos

2 c. lard or shortening
1 c. sugar
1 t. anise seed or cinnamon
2 eggs
6 c. sifted flour
3 t. baking powder
1 t. salt
1/4 c. water, white wine or dry sherry
1/2 c. sugar
1 t. cinnamon

Cream shortening thoroughly. Add sugar and anise seed or cinnamon. Add eggs to mixture and beat until fluffy. Sift flour with baking powder and salt; add to first mixture. Add water and knead until well mixed. Roll to 1/4" on lightly floured board and cut into fancy shapes. May be put through cookie press. Mix together the sugar and cinnamon; sprinkle on top of cookies. Bake in 350 oven 8-10 minutes, until lightly browned. Makes 4-6 dozen cookies.

Reflections on Ethnic Backgrounds

M E ❧ N U

Isabel Hovel, President
North Dakota State Federation of Garden Clubs

Mulled Apple Cider
Smothered Pheasant*
Stovies*

German-Russian Soup*
German Cucumber Salad*
Rhubarb Cream Pie*

German-Russian Soup

4-5 medium potatoes
1 medium onion, chopped
1 celery stalk, chopped
1 carrot, sliced
2 c. flour
2 t. baking powder
1 t. salt
2 eggs
1/2 c. water or milk
1 can cream of chicken soup
1 c. milk or cream

Peel and cube potatoes in 1" cubes. Put in saucepot with enough water to cover. Add vegetables. Boil until semi done. To make dumplings, combine flour, baking powder, salt, eggs and water or milk. Roll dough into logs of 1/2" diameter. Cut the logs into approximately 1/2" lengths. Drop into the boiling potatoes and simmer until the dumplings are tender, about 10-12 minutes. Add can cream of chicken soup mixed with milk or cream. Stir until hot.

Smothered Pheasant

1 ring-necked pheasant
Oil or shortening
1 c. light cream

Prepare and panfry same as fried chicken. Add cream and cover and simmer 1-1/2 hours or bake at 325 until tender.

German Cucumber Salad

2 cucumbers, sliced
2 t. salt
1/2 c. vinegar
1/2 c. water
1 c. whipping or sour cream
1/2 t. sugar (optional)
Pepper or white pepper to taste (optional)

In bowl, mix cucumber, salt and enough water to cover. Let set for 2 or more hours in the refrigerator. Drain off the salt water thoroughly. Mix together the vinegar and water. Put the cucumbers in and let set several hours or overnight in the refrigerator. Drain most, but not all of the vinegar off and add rest of the ingredients.

Stovies

6 large potatoes, peeled and thinly sliced
2 medium onions, peeled and thinly sliced
1/3 c. butter, margarine, bacon fat or chicken fat
Salt and pepper to taste
1 c. water or stock

Arrange potatoes and onions in layers in a heavy pan. Dot each layer with the desired fat. Sprinkle with salt and pepper. Add water or stock. Cover; simmer gently until potato is soft. May add crumbled bacon or small chunks of ham.

Rhubarb Cream Pie

Pastry enough for 2 crust pie
4 c. fresh rhubarb, cut into 1" chunks
2 c. sugar
3/4 t. nutmeg
3 eggs
3 T. milk, cream or evaporated milk
3 T. cornstarch or 1/4 c. flour
1 T. butter or margarine

Combine fruit, sugar and nutmeg. Mix eggs, liquids and cornstarch or flour and add to the mix. Pour into unbaked pastry lined 9" pie pan. Dot with butter. Top with a lattice pastry top. Brush with cream and sprinkle with sugar, if desired. Bake at 425 for 40-50 minutes.

Quick, I've Been Gone All Day to Garden Club Meetings....

M E N U

Judi Starr, President
The Garden Club of Ohio, Inc.

Cuban Black Bean Soup Supper*
Rice in a Rush with Pecans*
Quick I've Been Gone All Day to
Garden Club Meetings Chicken*   with Citrus Sauce*
Mixed Greens Salad   Chocolate Ice Cream

Cuban Black Bean Soup Supper

1 lb. dried black beans
2 qt. water
1-1/2 T. salt
5 oz. Spanish olive oil
4-5 cloves garlic, finely minced
1/2 T. cumin
1-1/2 t. dried oregano
2 T. balsamic or red wine vinegar
1/2 lb. onions, finely chopped
1/2 c. red sweet pepper, minced
1/2 of one chipotle pepper in adobe sauce (optional)
1-2 T. adobe sauce (optional)
1 T. cream sherry (optional)
4 dollops sour cream
4 thin slices of lemon, seeds removed
1/4 c. rice

Soak washed beans in water overnight. Add salt and cook beans in water   until tender but not soft.   Chop garlic and add cumin, oregano and vinegar.   Set aside. Cut onions and peppers into very small pieces. Heat oil in pan and sauté pepper mixture with the adobe sauce until lightly brown. Add garlic mixture, sauté slowly until mixture produces fragrant scent and is rich red-brown in color. Set aside. Drain some water from the cooked beans and combine sautéed vegetable mixture. Cook slowly until ready to serve. Add cream sherry about 10 minutes before serving. Cook rice. To serve, spoon soup into bowls, and add 1/4 cup cooked rice, small dollop sour cream and one very thin lemon slice to top.

Rice in a Rush

1/2 c. wild rice
2 chopped mushrooms
1 c. white or brown rice
1/4 c. pecans
1/2 c. parsley, chopped

Cook wild rice and mushrooms together according to package instructions.   Cook white or brown rice in another pan according to instructions. Mix both rices with pecans and parsley when ready to serve.

Quick
I've Been at Garden Club Meetings All Day
Boneless Chicken Breasts with Citrus Sauce

2 T. vegetable oil
3 whole chicken breasts, skinless, boned and halved
2 egg whites and 1 egg yolk
3/4 c. flour
1 T. Old Bay seasoning

In heavy skillet, heat oil until very hot but not smoking. Whisk eggs until fluffy. In separate bowl, combine flour and seasoning. Dip all chicken into egg mixture, set aside in pie plate until all pieces are dipped. Lightly dip chicken into flour mixture and immediately place into very hot oil. Cook quickly until golden brown. Do not cover skillet. Turn once. Serve immediately with citrus sauce on side.

Citrus Sauce

1/4 c. orange juice
1 T. frozen orange juice concentrate
1/4 c. lime juice
1/4 c. lemon juice
3-4 T. corn starch
Slivers of orange or lemon zest

Stir all juices together. Add slowly to cornstarch, stirring to prevent lumping, before putting onto heat. Cook slowly, stirring constantly with wooden spoon, in small skillet or pan just until clear and cornstarch flavor is gone, about 3-4 minutes. If it gets too thick, remove from heat and add more frozen concentrate. Pour some over cooked chicken breasts. Save some to serve.

Low Fat and Low Sugar Dinner

M E N U

Marjorie Franklin, President
Oklahoma Garden Clubs, Inc.

Garlic-Herb Dip*	Low Fat Tostitos
Fat Free Pretzel Chips	Eggplant Casserole*
Tossed Salad	Orange Jell-O Salad*
Dilly Bread*	Angel Food Cake

Garlic-Herb Dip

2 c. low-fat cottage cheese
2/3 c. milk
2 T. fresh or 1 T. dried parsley
Pinch curry powder
1/8 t. paprika
1/2 t. basil
1/2 clove garlic
1 small red cabbage

Place cottage cheese, milk, spices and garlic in blender or food processor. Process until smooth. Hollow out the head of cabbage from the top. Cut a slice from the stem end so the cabbage will rest firmly on its base, use as a bowl for dip.

Eggplant Casserole

2 medium eggplants
2 eggs, beaten
3 c. tomatoes, canned
4 T. melted butter
2 small onions, chopped
1 c. grated American cheese
1 lb. cooked, crumbled, hamburger meat (optional)
2 c. dried bread crumbs, buttered

Peel eggplant, cut into cubes and cook 7 minutes in salt water. Drain and place in 8x13" baking dish. Mix rest of ingredients, but save 1 cup of buttered bread crumbs and grated cheese for top. Add cooked hamburger, if using. Pour on the eggplant and add grated cheese and sprinkle with remaining bread crumbs. Bake at 375 for 45 minutes or until heated through and cheese is melted.

Jell-O Salad

3 small boxes orange Jell-O
1 small box lemon Jell-O
1 small can frozen orange juice concentrate
2 cans Mandarin orange segments
1 can crushed pineapple

Dissolve Jell-O in 1 cup hot water, slightly cool, add frozen juice. When dissolved add pineapple and Mandarin oranges. Add cold water until Jell-O equals required liquid. Pour into mold.

Dilly Casserole Bread

1 packet dry yeast or 1 cake yeast
1/4 c. warm water
1 c. creamed cottage cheese, heated to lukewarm
2 T. sugar
1/4 c. instant minced onion
1 T. margarine
2 t. dill seed
1 t. salt
1/4 t. baking soda
1 unbeaten egg
2-1/4 to 2-1/2 c. sifted flour

Soften yeast in water. Combine cottage cheese, sugar, onion, margarine, dill seed, salt, baking soda, egg and softened yeast. Add flour to form a stiff dough. Let rise in warm place until light and doubled in size, 50-60 minutes. Stir down dough; turn into a well greased 8" round casserole. Let rise in warm place until light, 30-40 minutes. Bake in a 350 oven 40-50 minutes until crust is dark brown. Brush with soft margarine and sprinkle with salt.

Dutch Baby German Pancakes

3 eggs
3/4 c. milk
3/4 c. flour
1/2 stick butter
Nutmeg

Heat oven to 425. In an iron skillet, melt the butter until it starts to bubble. While skillet is heating, in a blender add eggs; blend one minute.   Add milk, then slowly add flour, blending for another minute or so. Add fresh grated nutmeg to taste. Pour batter into hot butter in skillet.   Bake 10-12 minutes. Batter will creep up sides of skillet and puff up. Turn out on large platter. Can top with any or all of the following toppings: syrup, sour cream, whipped cream, any fresh fruit, powdered sugar, etc. Serve immediately. Serves 2-3.

Apple Dutch Baby

Follow recipe for Dutch Baby German Pancakes. Add 2 additional tablespoons butter to skillet, 1/4 cup brown sugar, 1 crisp apple sliced and tossed with 2 teaspoons cinnamon. This is great served with sour cream.

Menu from Rhode Island

M E ❈ N U

Frankie Nannig, President
The Rhode Island Federation of Garden Clubs, Inc.

Rhode Island Clam Cakes* and Chowder*
Baked Stuffed Lobster*   Rhode Island Johnny Cakes*
Sunshine Salad   Indian Pudding à la Mode*

Rhode Island Clam Cakes

1-1/2 c. flour
1-1/2 t. baking powder
1/2 t. salt
1 T. sugar
1/4 t. paprika
1 egg
1 c. clam juice with chopped clams
1 T. vegetable oil

Mix first 7 ingredients and drop by spoonful into hot vegetable oil.
Fry until golden.

Rhode Island Clam Chowder

1/2 lb. salt pork
2 large onions, chopped
6 large potatoes, peeled and diced
4 c. clam juice
2 c. chopped clams

Slice salt pork, sauté in a large pot until rendered, add chopped onions, sauté until golden. Add diced potato and clam juice to cover potato. May add some water if you do not have enough juice. Bring to a slow boil, over medium heat and cook until potatoes are almost done, about 15 minutes. Remove salt pork. Add chopped clams, bring to a boil for just a minute. Simmer until ready to serve. Serve hot.

Baked Stuffed Lobster

2 live lobsters, 1-1/2 to 2 lb. each
2-1/2 c. bread crumbs
1 onion, finely chopped
1 celery stalk, chopped
Scallops or small shrimp (optional)
White wine
Bread crumbs
1/2 c. butter, melted

Slit lobsters open from underside, remove sack near head and discard. Add roe and tamale into the stuffing. Select an oven-proof pan such as a lasagna pan. Place lobsters in pan. Mix other ingredients in a bowl, using enough white wine to moisten the stuffing. Press stuffing into lobster body cavity; cover with crumbs, spoon 1/2 cup melted butter on top of crumbs. Add 1-1/2 cups water to pan. Cover with aluminum foil and press around edges to seal pan. Bake lobsters in preheated 425 oven for 35 minutes. Slit foil with fork to remove steam. Remove foil from pan and return pan to oven for about 5 minutes. Serve with melted butter and lemon.

Rhode Island Johnny Cakes

1 c. ground white cornmeal
1/2 c. boiling water
1/2 c. milk
Salt and pepper to taste

Stir boiling water into cornmeal. Add milk until smooth. Salt and pepper; drop by large spoonfuls on hot greased griddle. Cook to golden brown on both sides. Serve buttered with milk or maple syrup.

Indian Pudding à la Mode

2 c. milk
1-1/2 T. Indian meal or cornmeal
3 eggs, well beaten
1 pint cold milk
1 T. flour
1/2 c. sugar
1/2 c. molasses
1 t. ginger
1 t. cinnamon
1 pinch salt

Boil milk and stir in cornmeal. Add remaining ingredients and place in greased baking dish. Bake at 350 for 1 hour or until set. Serve warm topped with a scoop of vanilla ice cream.

Family Christmas Day Buffet

M E ❧ N U

Donna Marsh, President
The Garden Club of South Carolina, Inc.

Aunt Fay's Punch*   Ron's Christmas Party Mix*
Turkey and Ham Platters with Horseradish Sauce*
Layered Avocado Dip*
Five Bean Salad*   Crab Mousse*
Broccoli-Rice Casserole*   Heavenly Potatoes*
Crockpot Macaroni Pie*   Spicy Applesauce Mold*
Lime Mallow Mousse*   Craig's Pound Cake*

Aunt Fay's Punch

1 fifth Canada House Blended Whiskey
1 quart club soda
2 bottles Meijers white grape juice

Pour all of the above at once into a punch bowl with an ice ring
made of fruit or flowers Makes 4 quarts.

Ron's Christmas Party Mix

6 c. popped corn
1 6 oz. bag corn chips
2 c. bite-size pretzels
1 c. sunflower seeds
1 3 oz. can chow mein noodles
1 stick margarine
2 t. Worcestershire Sauce
1/2 t. hot pepper sauce
1 clove garlic, crushed

Mix popped corn, corn chips, pretzels, sunflower seeds and noodles in a large roasting pan. In a saucepan, melt margarine and stir in sauces and garlic. Pour over popcorn mixture and toss to mix well. Bake at 250 for 1 hour, stirring at 15 minute intervals to mix well during baking. Cool and store in airtight container.

Turkey and Ham Platters with Horseradish Sauce

1 large honey baked ham, sliced
1 large turkey, roasted and sliced thin
Small red spiced canned apples (optional)
Fresh curly parsley heads (optional)
8 oz. sour cream
2 T. milk
1-1/2 T. prepared horseradish

Arrange meat on a large platter, alternating slices of ham and turkey. Canned apples may be placed around the meat platter on top of parsley heads. Mix sour cream, milk and horseradish together and stir well. Place in bowl next to meat platter for easy access.

Layered Avocado Dip

2 ripe avocados, peeled and mashed
1/4 t. salt
1/2 t. lemon juice
1 c. sour cream
1 c. tomatoes, finely chopped
1/2 pkg. taco seasoning mix
1 c. Monterey Jack cheese, shredded
1 c. sharp cheddar cheese, shredded
1/4 c. black olives, chopped
1/4 c. green onions, chopped
1 t. hot pepper sauce

Combine avocado, salt and lemon juice and spread in bottom of round platter. Combine sour cream and taco seasoning mix. Spread over avocado mixture. Layer Monterey Jack and cheddar cheeses over sour cream mixture and pat down. Add tomatoes and sprinkle liberally with hot pepper sauce. Top with black olives and green onions. Serve with tortilla chips for dipping.

Five Bean Salad

1 c. lima beans, drained
1 c. wax beans, drained
1 c. French green beans, drained
1 c. butter beans, drained
1 c. kidney beans, drained
1 red onion, chopped
1-1/2 c. vinegar
1/2 c. water
2 c. sugar
1 t. salt

Mix beans together. In a saucepan, bring vinegar, water, sugar and salt to a rolling boil and pour over drained beans. Add onions. Cool before serving. Serves 10.

Crab Mousse

2 env. unflavored gelatin
1/4 c. cold water
1/2 c. boiling water
1 8 oz. cream cheese, softened
1 can cream of mushroom soup
1 c. mayonnaise
1 c. green onion, chopped
1 c. celery, chopped
Juice of 1 lemon
1 T. Worcestershire sauce
1 t. Old Port Republic Lemon Hot Sauce
1/2 c. stuffed olives, sliced
2 cans white crabmeat
Parsley for garnish

Soak gelatin in cold water. Add boiling water. In mixing bowl, mix cream cheese with mushroom soup; add remaining ingredients except parsley. Add gelatin, mix all together and place in ring mold. Will fill 2 four-cup molds. Chill. Unmold on serving plate and serve with crackers of choice. Decorate with parsley around and inside of ring mold. Serves 10.

Broccoli-Rice Casserole

1 c. minute rice, uncooked
1 c. water
1/2 c. onion, chopped
1/2 c. celery, chopped
1/2 stick margarine
1 can cream of mushroom soup
1 pkg. frozen chopped broccoli, thawed
3/4 c. cheddar cheese, grated

Combine all ingredients except cheddar cheese. Place in a glass casserole dish and scatter cheese on top. Bake 350 for 1 hour. Serves 10.

Heavenly Potatoes

24 oz. frozen shredded hash brown potatoes, thawed
1 can cream of chicken soup
1-3/4 c. mild cheddar cheese, grated
1 stick margarine, melted
1 t. salt
1/4 t. pepper
1 pint sour cream
1 medium onion, chopped
Crushed cornflakes (optional)
Margarine, melted (optional)

Mix first 8 ingredients together and put in greased 9x13" baking dish. May top with crushed cornflakes mixed with melted margarine. Bake at 350 for 45 minutes.

Crockpot Macaroni Pie

8 oz. macaroni, cooked and drained
1-1/2 c. milk
1 can evaporated milk
1 t. salt
2 c. sharp cheddar cheese, shredded
1 c. mild cheddar cheese, shredded
1/4 c. margarine, melted
2 eggs
1/4 t. black pepper
4-6 cheese slices

Mix all ingredients together except cheese slices. Put into greased crockpot. Lay cheese slices on top and sprinkle with paprika. Cook 3-4 hours on low setting. Serves 8.

Spicy Applesauce Mold

1/2 c. red cinnamon candies
1 c. water
1 6 oz. pkg. raspberry Jell-O
2 15 oz. cans applesauce
2 T. vinegar
Endive, garnish
Orange slices, garnish

Cook candies in a cup water, stirring frequently until melted. Heat to boiling, pour over gelatin in large bowl, stir until gelatin dissolves. Stir in applesauce and vinegar. Pour into 6 cup mold and refrigerate until firm. Unmold onto serving plate, garnishing with endive and orange slices. Serves 10.

Lime Mallow Mousse

1 pkg. lime Jell-O
1 c. boiling water
1/2 c. small marshmallows
1 c. ginger ale
1 small can crushed pineapple, drained, saving liquid
2 bananas, sliced
1 egg beaten
1/2 c. sugar
2 T. butter, softened
2 T. flour
1 pkg. Dream Whip topping mix

Dissolve Jell-O in water and add marshmallows. When almost cool, add ginger ale. Put in Jell-O mold and place in refrigerator. When slightly thickened, add pineapple and bananas. When completely set, place egg, sugar, butter and flour in a saucepan. Add 1 cup of the reserved pineapple juice, adding water if needed, to make 1 cup. Cook over medium heat to custard consistency, stirring constantly. Cool and frost over Jell-O mold. Chill well. Unmold. Prepare Dream Whip topping according to directions. Spread on top of Jell-O. Serves 10.

Craig's Pound Cake

1 box yellow cake mix
1 box instant pineapple cream pudding
3/4 c. oil
3/4 c. cold water
2 T. fresh orange juice
4 eggs

Beat cake mix, pudding, oil, cold water and orange juice together. Add eggs one at a time, beating after each egg. Beat 2 minutes more. Put in a greased and floured angel food cake pan. Bake at 350 for 50 minutes. Do not open oven door until done. Serves 10.

Pheasant Dinner

M E N U

Dr. Lynn Olson, President
South Dakota Federation of Garden Clubs, Inc.

Clear Soup   Blueberry-Radish Salad*
Pheasant Breasts Piquant*   Barley Casserole*
Broccoli Casserole   Rolls and Butter
Sherry Creme Pears*

Blueberry-Radish Salad

1 t. grated orange rind
Juice of 1 orange
1/3 c. oil
2 T. minced parsley
Salt and freshly ground white pepper
6 c. torn escarole or mixed greens
1-1/2 c. coarsely shredded radishes
1 c. fresh blueberries

Combine and mix first 4 ingredients well. Season with salt and white pepper. Put escarole or mixed greens in bowl. Top with radishes, then sprinkle with blueberries. Just before serving add dressing and toss. Makes 6 servings.

Pheasant Breasts Piquant

3 pheasant or chicken breasts, split in 1/2
3/4 c. rosé wine
1 clove garlic, diced
1/4 c. soy sauce
1 t. ginger
1/4 c. salad oil
1/2 t. oregano
2 T. water
1 T. brown sugar

Arrange pheasant or chicken breasts in baking dish. Mix remaining ingredients together and pour over breasts. Cover and bake at 325 for 1-1/2 hours. Serve over brown and wild rice if desired.

Barley Casserole

1 c. pearl barley
1/4 c. butter
1 grated onion
1 can chicken broth
1 env. dry onion soup
1 c. almonds, slivered
1 can mushrooms with liquid

Brown barley in butter in saucepan. Add remaining ingredients, place in casserole dish and bake covered at 325 for 1-1/2 hours.

Sherry Creme Pears

2 16 oz. cans Bartlett pear halves
2 3 oz. pkgs. cream cheese, softened
3 T. powdered sugar
2 T. pecans, chopped
1/4 t. almond extract
Green Maraschino cherries for garnish
1 3-1/8 oz. pkg. vanilla pudding, not instant
1-1/4 c. milk
1 c. pear syrup
1/4 c. sherry

Drain pears, reserving 1 cup pear syrup. Blend softened cream cheese with powdered sugar, pecans and almond extract. Spread mixture over cut sides of 6 pear halves, carefully covering entire surface. Top each with another pear half, pressing gently. Stand each pair of pear halves upright in a stemmed dessert dish if available. Garnish with pieces of maraschino cherries to resemble leaves and stem. Combine pudding mix with milk and reserved 1 cup pear syrup. Cook and stir over medium heat until mixture boils. Remove from heat and add sherry. Cool slightly. Pour around pears. Chill until ready to serve. Makes 6 desserts.

Menu from Tennessee

M E N U

Mrs. Laury K. Weaver, Jr., President
Tennessee Federation of Garden Clubs, Inc.

Lobster Bisque*   Fresh Garden Salad
Rock Cornish Hens*   Nutted Wild Rice*
Fresh Asparagus with Hollandaise   Yeast Breads
Fresh Raspberry Chocolate Shortcake*

Lobster Bisque

2-1/2 c. chicken stock
1 sliced onion
4 ribs of celery with leaves
2 whole cloves
1 bay leaf
6 peppercorns
1/4 c. butter
1/4 c. flour
3 c. milk
1/4 t. nutmeg
Meat from 2 medium boiled lobsters
1 c. cream
Minced parsley
Dash paprika
Dash dry sherry

Place chicken stock, onion, celery, cloves, bay leaf and peppercorns in large pot. Simmer for 1/2 hour, strain stock. In another pot, melt butter, stir in flour. Gradually add milk and nutmeg. When sauce is smooth and boiling add the lobster and stock. Simmer bisque, covered, for 5 minutes. Turn off heat and stir in cream. Serve at once with parsley, paprika and sherry. Makes about 6 cups.

Rock Cornish Hens

6 fresh rock cornish hens
1/2 stick butter, softened
Seasoned salt
Freshly ground pepper
Paprika
Watercress for garnish

Preheat oven to 350. Rinse hens well under cold running water and pat dry. Truss and rub with butter, sprinkle with salt, pepper and paprika. Arrange hens in a shallow roasting pan just large enough to hold them or use 2 smaller baking dishes. Bake for about 1 hour, basting frequently, until hens are golden brown and done. Transfer to serving platter and garnish with watercress. Remove grease from sauce in roasting pan and reduce over medium heat to 2/3 the amount. Serve sauce on the side.

Nutted Wild Rice

1 c. raw wild rice
5-1/2 c. chicken stock or water
1 c. shelled pecan halves
1 c. yellow raisins
Grated rind of a large orange
1/4 c. chopped fresh mint
4 scallions, thinly sliced
1/4 c. olive oil
1/3 c. fresh orange juice
1-1/2 t. salt
Freshly ground black pepper to taste

Rinse rice under cold water thoroughly. Place rice in a medium saucepan. Add stock or water and bring to a rapid boil. Adjust heat to a gentle simmer and cook uncovered for 45 minutes. After 30 minutes check for doneness; rice should not be too soft. Place a thin towel inside a colander and turn rice into the colander to drain. Transfer drained rice to a bowl. Add remaining ingredients to rice and toss gently. Let mixture stand for 2 hours to allow flavor to develop. Serve at room temperature. Serves 6.

Fresh Raspberry Chocolate Shortcake

1/2 c. butter or margarine, softened
1-1/4 c. sugar
2 large eggs, separated
1-1/4 c. sifted cake flour
2 t. baking powder
1/4 t. salt
1/3 c. cocoa
2/3 c. milk
1 t. vanilla extract

2 T. seedless raspberry jam
2 T. Chambord or other raspberry flavored liqueur
2 c. whipping cream
1/4 c. sifted confectioner's sugar
3 c. fresh raspberries
Fresh mint sprigs for garnish

Grease two 9" round cake pans; line with waxed paper and grease. Set aside. Beat butter at medium speed with an electric mixer 2 minutes or until creamy. Add sugar gradually, beating well. Add egg yolks, one at a time, beating until blended after each addition. Combine flour and next 3 ingredients; add to butter mixture alternately with milk, beginning and ending with flour mixture. Beat at low speed until blended after each addition. Stir in vanilla. Beat egg whites at high speed with an electric mixer until stiff peaks form; gently fold into batter. Pour batter into prepared pans. Bake at 350 for 18 minutes or until a wooden pick inserted in center comes out clean. Cool in pans on wire racks 10 minutes. Remove from pans; cool completely on wire racks. Cook jam in a small saucepan over low heat until melted; stir in liqueur. Set jam mixture aside. Beat whipping cream at medium speed with an electric mixer until foamy; gradually add powdered sugar, beating until soft peaks form. Place one cake layer on a serving plate; brush with half of jam mixture. Arrange half of raspberries over jam. Spread half of whipped cream over raspberries. Top with second cake layer. Brush with remaining jam mixture. Spread remaining whipped cream over jam mixture. Arrange remaining raspberries on top. Garnish, if desired.

Texas Summer Supper

M E ✿ N U

Jayne Martin, President
Texas Garden Clubs, Inc.

King Ranch Chicken*
Mixed Fresh Vegetable Salad with Avocado
Flan*

King Ranch Chicken

3-4 lb. broiler-fryer
1 onion
2 ribs celery
Salt and pepper
1 onion, chopped
1 large bell pepper, chopped
1 can cream of mushroom soup
1 can cream of chicken soup
1/2-3/4 lb. cheddar cheese, grated
Chili powder
Garlic salt
18 corn tortillas, frozen
1 can tomatoes and green chiles, undrained

Boil chicken until tender, in water to cover, seasoned with onion, celery, salt and pepper. Drain, reserving liquid. Cut chicken into bite-sized pieces. Combine onion and bell pepper. Combine soups and mix with a little of the stock until it is of spreading consistency. Heat stock until boiling and continue to boil over medium heat as you dip each frozen tortilla into it to wilt. It should take 15-20 seconds each. Start layering casserole in a 9x12" baking dish in this order: tortillas, dripping with stock, chicken, onion and bell pepper, chili powder and garlic salt to taste, soup mixture, and cheese. Repeat the layers, making sure that the tortillas are oozing with the stock. Cover the casserole with the canned tomatoes and green chiles. If the juices in the casserole are not up to 1/2 the depth of the dish, add more of the chicken stock. Bake uncovered at 375 for 30-40 minutes. Serves 8-10. Best if made a day ahead and refrigerated to let the flavors blend.

Flan

1 c. sugar
4 eggs, separated
1 can sweetened condensed milk
Same amount of whole milk, 1% or 2%
1 t. vanilla

In top of double boiler, add sugar and heat over direct high heat until caramelized. Pour into ring mold, tilting pan from side to side to coat sides and bottom of pan. In a large bowl, beat egg white until stiff; add egg yolks, one at a time, beating well after each addition. Add condensed milk, whole milk and vanilla. Beat thoroughly. Pour mixture over caramelized sugar. Place ring mold in a shallow pan of hot water and bake in 350 oven until toothpick comes out clean, approximately 40-60 minutes.

Homer's Buttermilk Pancake Breakfast

M E ❦ N U

Earlene Hale, President
The Utah Associated Garden Clubs, Inc.

Fresh Fruit Compote
Homer's Buttermilk Pancakes*
Bacon   Sausage

Homer's Buttermilk Pancakes
1 c. flour
1 T. sugar
1/2 t. baking soda
2 t. baking powder
1 c. buttermilk
1 egg
1 T. cooking oil
1/2 c. water

Mix flour, sugar, baking soda and baking powder together in large bowl. Add rest of ingredients, adding more water if needed. Let batter sit for 10 minutes to form bubbles. Cook on very hot griddle.

Simple Menu for Entertaining

M E N U

Jane Lundblad, President
West Virginia Garden Clubs, Inc.

Chicken Delight*	Steamed Rice
Steamed Broccoli	Layered Salad*
Hot bread or rolls	Triple Lemon Treat*

Chicken Delight

1 8 oz. jar apricot or peach preserves, or orange marmalade
1 pkg. dry onion soup
1 small bottle Catalina salad dressing
Chicken pieces to serve 6-8 people

Place chicken in baking pan. Mix above ingredients and pour over chicken. Bake at 350 for 1 to 1-1/2 hours. Watch carefully and cover with foil if browning too quickly.

Layered Salad

1 small head iceberg lettuce, or greens of your choice
2 ribs celery, sliced thin
1 sweet onion, sliced thin
1 c. mayonnaise
1 T. vinegar
1/2 c. sour cream
1/3 c. sugar
4 slices bacon, fried crisp and crumbled
Parmesan cheese

In serving bowl, layer lettuce, then celery, then onion. Mix mayonnaise and vinegar together and spread over top, sealing to edges. Mix sour cream and sugar together and drizzle over top. Sprinkle bacon on top and then Parmesan cheese. Cover and refrigerate for at least 1 hour.

Triple Lemon Treat

1/2 c. margarine, softened
1 c. flour
1 8 oz. pkg. cream cheese
1 c. confectioner's sugar
1 13-1/2 oz. container whipped topping
2 3-3/4 oz. pkgs. lemon instant pudding and pie filling
3 c. cold milk
Lemon juice
Chopped pecans or lemon slices

Blend margarine into flour with pastry blender until consistency of coarse crumbs. Press into 9x13x2" pan. Bake at 350 for 10 minutes. Cool. Combine cream cheese and sugar. Mix until smooth. Fold in whipped topping, reserving 1 cup. Spread mixture over cooled pastry. Combine pudding mix and milk. Beat until smooth and thickened. Add lemon juice if more tartness is desired. Spread over cream cheese layer. Spread reserved topping over top and sprinkle with pecan pieces or garnish with lemon slices. Refrigerate.

Czech Delight

M E N U

Barbara Wesley, President
Wisconsin Garden Club Federation

Roasted Pork Loin*   Potato Dumplings*
Sauerkraut Surprise*   Cranberries Continental*
Dilly Batter Bread*   Poppyseed Layer Cake*

Roasted Pork Loin

2-1/2 - 3 lb. boneless pork loin
Salt, pepper and caraway seed

Season pork loin with salt, pepper and caraway seed. Roast at 350
for 30 minutes per pound or until thermometer measures 160.
May make gravy using brown drippings from pan; add chicken
broth and cornstarch and season to taste with additional salt, pepper, paprika and kitchen bouquet.

Potato Dumplings

4 medium potatoes, cooked and mashed
2 eggs
2 t. salt
1/4 c. dry cream of wheat
2 or more c. flour

Chill potatoes. Knead all ingredients together; form into large egg shaped balls, flouring hands if necessary. Put into boiling water. Simmer for 25 minutes. Dumplings will float to the top.

Sauerkraut Surprise

1 large can sauerkraut, drained, rinsed and drained again
1/2 lb. bacon, minced
2 onions, diced
1 lb. fresh mushrooms, sliced

Fry bacon and onions together over medium heat, stirring occasionally. Add mushrooms and sauerkraut. Cover and cook slowly about 15 minutes.

Cranberries Continental

1 orange, minced, with peel on
1 stick cinnamon
3 cloves stuck in orange peel triangles
1/2 c. water
2 c. sugar
4 c. cranberries
4 c. brandy

In saucepan, bring orange, cinnamon, orange peel triangles and water to a boil. Simmer, covered, for 10 minutes. Add sugar and cranberries. Simmer until cranberries pop. Remove from heat and add brandy. Remove clove triangles and cinnamon stick before storing. Improves with age. Can be frozen.

Dilly Batter Bread

3-1/4 c. all purpose flour
2 pkgs. dry yeast
2 T. sugar
2 t. dill seed
1 T. instant or fresh minced onion
1 t. salt
1 c. water
8 oz. plain yogurt
2 T. shortening
1 egg

In medium bowl, combine 1-1/2 cups flour, yeast, sugar, onion, dill seed and salt. Heat water, yogurt and shortening until warm, 120-130. Shortening does not have to melt. Add to flour mixture. Add egg. Blend at low speed until moistened, beat 3 minutes at medium speed. Gradually stir in remaining flour to make a stiff batter. Spoon into greased 1-1/2 - 2 quart casserole dish. Cover. Raise until doubled, about 1 hour. Bake at 375 for 30-40 minutes, or until golden brown. Serve warm or cold. Makes 1 round loaf.

Poppyseed Layer Cake

1 c. poppyseed
3/4 c. milk
1/2 c. butter
1-1/2 c. sugar
1 t. vanilla
2 c. flour
2 t. baking powder
1/2 c. milk
3 egg whites, beaten stiff

Soak poppyseed in 3/4 c. milk overnight. Cream butter, sugar and vanilla.   Sift flour and baking powder together.   Alternately add flour, 1/2 cup milk and poppyseed mixture into creamed butter. Fold in egg whites. Bake in 2 greased 9" layer pans at 350. Test after 20 minutes with toothpick.

Filling:
1 c. sugar
2 T. cornstarch
1 c. milk
Juice and rind of 1 lemon
3 egg yolks, beaten
1 T. butter

Combine all ingredients, except butter, in saucepan. Cook over low heat until thick. Add butter. Cool and put in between cooled cake layers.

Frosting:
4 T. flour
1 c. milk
1 c. butter
1 c. sugar
1 t. vanilla

Cook flour and milk until thick. Cover and chill. Cream butter and sugar; add vanilla. Add chilled flour mixture 1 tablespoon at a time. Whip 10 minutes, scraping bowl occasionally. Frost top and sides of cake.

Oriental Beef Balls
with Ralph's Favorite Dessert
M E ❦ N U

Betty Updike, President
Wyoming Federation of Garden Clubs, Inc.

Oriental Beef Balls*   with Sweet & Sour Sauce*
Rice   Ralph's Favorite Dessert*

Oriental Beef Balls

1 lb. ground lean beef
2 T. onion, finely chopped
1/2 c. fine dry bread crumbs
1 T. parsley, chopped
1/4 t. garlic salt
1/8 t. pepper
1 egg
2/3 c. milk
2 T. vegetable oil
1/8 t. curry powder

Mix first 8 ingredients together until well blended. Cover and chill an hour or longer; shape into about 32 small meat balls. In large electric, or other skillet, heat oil and curry powder. Brown meat balls slowly on all sides. Drain off fat.

Sweet and Sour Sauce

1 13-1/2 oz. can pineapple tidbits, drained, reserving syrup
1/4 c. vinegar
1/4 c. sugar
1 T. cornstarch
1 T. soy sauce
1 7 oz. pkg. frozen Chinese pea pods

In saucepan, add 1/2 cup syrup drained from pineapple, vinegar, sugar, cornstarch and soy sauce. Cook over low heat until sauce thickens and clears. Pour sauce over meat balls and cook over low heat, stirring gently. In saucepan, pour boiling water over frozen pea pods; cover and let stand 5 minutes. Drain pea pods and add to meat balls along with drained pineapple tidbits. Stir and heat to serving temperature. Serve over cooked rice. Serves four or more.

Ralph's Favorite Dessert

18 vanilla wafers, crushed
1 c. chocolate chips
6 T. confectioner's sugar
3 T. water
3 egg yolks
3 egg whites, stiffly beaten
1 c. walnuts, chopped
1 t, vanilla
1/2 pint whipping cream, whipped

Put half of vanilla wafer crumbs in bottom of oiled 8x8" pan. In double boiler, stir chocolate chips, confectioner's sugar and water together; stir in egg yolks, one at a time. Set aside to cool. When cool, stir in egg whites, walnuts, vanilla and whipped cream. Pour over wafer crumbs in pan. Sprinkle rest of crumbs on top. Refrigerate or freeze. Cut in squares to serve. To serve as a chocolate mousse, pour mixture into tall glasses, refrigerate and serve with a dollop of whipped cream on top.

The SIDEBOARD

The Garden Club of Kentucky, Inc.
Menus from Board of Directors
and Club Members

Sarah G. Pursifull
Favorite Luncheons
President, 1957-1959
The Garden Club of Kentucky, Inc......page 127

Joan Wipperman
Winter's Eve Delight
President, 1977-1979
The Garden Club of Kentucky, Inc......page 129

Jo Jean Scott
Luncheon on the Limoges
President, 1987-1989
The Garden Club of Kentucky, Inc......page 132

Carey Huddleston
Elegant But Easy Dinner For Six
President, 1989-1991
The Garden Club of Kentucky, Inc......page 136

Becky Oliver
Country Ham Dinner
President, 1991-1993
The Garden Club of Kentucky, Inc......page 139

Carolyn Roof
Carolyn's Quick and Easy Summer Menu
President, 1993-1995
The Garden Club of Kentucky, Inc......page 142

Martha Sims
Dining at the Sims
First Vice President GCKY
Fleming County Garden Club.....page 143

125

Favorite Luncheons

M E ❧ N U

Sarah G. Pursifull, President, 1957-1959
The Garden Club of Kentucky, Inc.
Country Ham on Beaten Biscuits
Tomato Filled with Chicken Salad*
Tomato Aspic Rings with Cottage Cheese*
Green Vegetable Casserole
Frozen Green Lima Beans
Hot Rolls
Raspberry Sherbet and Wafers
Chocolate Covered Mints

Tomato Aspic Rings

1 env. unflavored gelatin
1/4 c. cold water
1-1/2 c. V-8 Juice
1/4 t. salt and pinch of white pepper

In mixing bowl sprinkle gelatin over cold water and 1/2 cup of the V-8 Juice. Allow to soften for about 5 minutes. Heat the remaining juice to boiling point and add to gelatin. Add salt and pepper and stir until dissolved. Pour into 4-6 individual molds and chill. Unmold and serve on lettuce leaf.

Tomato Filled with Chicken Salad

1 large hen
1 T. lemon juice
Salt
1 c. chopped celery
1/2 c. blanched and toasted slivered almonds
1/2 c. chopped green olives
1/4 c. mayonnaise
4 medium size tomatoes

Boil hen until tender. When cooled, cut into bite size pieces and sprinkle with lemon juice and salt. Add celery, almonds and olives. Mix in mayonnaise and keep in the refrigerator until ready to serve. Cut the stem off the tomatoes and cut down, not quite through, in 5 or 6 wedges and spoon chicken on top.

Winter's Eve Delight

M E N U

Joan Wipperman, President, 1977-1979
The Garden Club of Kentucky, Inc.

Marinated Pork Tenderloin*
Mashed Potato Casserole*
Broccoli with Radishes*
Red Leaf Lettuce Salad*   Baked Custard*

Marinated Pork Tenderloin

3 lb. Pork Tenderloin
1 c. soy sauce
1 small jar orange marmalade

Marinate meat in soy sauce for 2 hours. Spread with orange marmalade before baking. Bake 325 for 1-1/2 to 2 hours or until thermometer registers 170.

Mashed Potato Casserole

5 lb. Potatoes, cooked and mashed
8 oz. cream cheese
1/2 stick butter
1/2 c. milk
2 eggs, slightly beaten
1/2 c. chopped onion
Salt and pepper

Stir cream cheese and butter into hot mashed potatoes. Stir milk, eggs and onion together and fold into mashed potatoes. Salt and pepper to taste. Spoon into a casserole dish and bake 45 minutes at 350.

Broccoli with Radishes

1 lb. fresh broccoli
4 red radishes
1 T. oil or butter

Wash and steam broccoli spears. Slice radishes and sauté in oil or butter. Serve over hot broccoli.

Red Leaf Lettuce Salad

1 bunch fresh red leaf lettuce
1 small box fresh strawberries
1/2 c. pecans
2 T. butter
2 T. brown sugar

Wash lettuce and tear. Place on individual salad plates. Wash and slice   fresh strawberries over lettuce. Sauté pecans in butter and brown sugar.   Let cool and separate. Top over salads.

Baked Custard

6 eggs, lightly beaten
6 T. sugar
4 c. milk, scalded
1 t. vanilla
Dash of nutmeg

Beat eggs and sugar together. Slowly stir in the scalded milk. Add vanilla and nutmeg. Bake in 8 individual cups, placed in a pan of hot water. Bake in 350ø oven for 30 minutes. Serve with fruit of the season.

Luncheon on the Limoges

M E ❧ N U

Jo Jean Scott, President, 1987-1989
The Garden Club of Kentucky, Inc.

Cheese Squares*   Shrimp and Seashells*
Chantilly Salad*   Summer Squash
Casserole*   Brown Sugar Carrots*
Parker House Rolls*

Cheese Squares

2 sticks soft butter
2 c. shredded cheddar cheese
1/2 c. grated onion
Cayenne pepper
Loaf of uncut, day-old bread
Paprika

Cream butter and cheese; add grated onion and a small amount of cayenne pepper. Slice bread and remove crust. Cut into 1-1/2" squares. Spread with cheese mixture and sprinkle with paprika. Bake at 350 for 10-12 minutes until golden. Serve warm. May be frozen before baking.

Shrimp and Seashells

1 lb. shrimp, boiled, shelled and chilled
3 hard-boiled eggs, chopped
1 c. finely chopped celery
1 c. mayonnaise
1 small box shell pasta, cooked and drained
Salt and pepper to taste

Toss together lightly and serve on a lettuce cup accompanied by a spiced peach, if desired.

Chantilly Salad

4 T. Knox gelatin
1 c. cold water
4 c. combined drained pineapple juice and water
1/2 c. vinegar
2 c. sugar
1 t. salt
1 can Royal Anne cherries, drained
1 large can pineapple chunks, drained and juice saved
2 cans grapefruit sections, drained

Dissolve the gelatin in the cold water. Add boiling juice/water combination, and stir well. Add sugar, salt and vinegar. Add well-drained fruit and let congeal in refrigerator in 9x13" glass dish. To serve, cut in squares and place on a leaf of lettuce; garnish with a bit of mayonnaise and touch of mint or sprinkle of paprika.

Summer Squash Casserole

6 to 8 medium yellow squash
Small onion, chopped
1/2 stick of butter
1 t. sugar
Salt and pepper to taste
Dash of seasoned salt
3 T. butter
3 T. flour
1-1/2 c. milk
1 c. shredded cheddar cheese
Buttered bread crumbs

Slice the squash and cook with the chopped onion in boiling water, until tender. Drain well. Season with butter, sugar, salt, pepper and seasoned salt. Mash. Make a medium white sauce by melting the butter and stirring in the flour. Remove from heat and stir in the milk. Return to heat and continue to stir until thickened. Add cheese and squash mixture. Place in a prepared casserole dish and sprinkle with buttered bread crumbs. Bake at 350 for about 20 minutes or until bubbly.

Brown Sugar Carrots

Several fresh carrots
1/2 stick of butter
1/4 c. brown sugar
Pinch of salt

Clean and slice carrots lengthwise into 3" pieces. Cook in boiling, lightly salted water, until tender. Drain. Remove carrots from saucepan. In same saucepan, melt butter and add the brown sugar. Stir until butter and sugar are well mixed. Gently place carrots back in the pan and stir to coat. Keep warm, over low heat, until time to serve.

Parker House Rolls

1 env. dry yeast
1/3 c. sugar
1/2 c. shortening
1/2 c. boiling water
1/2 c. cold water
1 egg, lightly beaten
3 c. unsifted flour
1/2 t. salt

Dissolve yeast in half cup of lukewarm water with 1 teaspoon sugar. Cream sugar and shortening; pour boiling water over. Mix in cold water and beaten egg. Add dissolved yeast. Sift flour and salt together over mixture and mix well. Cover with a damp tea towel and set in refrigerator overnight, keeping the tea towel damp. Place half of dough on a floured board and knead 4 times. Roll 1/4" thick. Cut with round cutter and spread with melted butter. Place on prepared cookie sheet and fold. Spread top with melted butter. Continue until all the dough is used. Let rise for 75 minutes. Bake at 450 for about 12 minutes or until golden brown.

Elegant But Easy Dinner for Six

M E ❧ N U

Carey Huddleston, President, 1989-1991
The Garden Club of Kentucky, Inc.

Carrots, Celery, Radishes and Olives   Shrimp Aspic*
Roast Leg of Lamb*   with Currant-Mint Sauce*
Buttered Peas or Lima Beans   Sweet Onion Casserole*
Trifle*

Shrimp Aspic

1 env. gelatin
1/4 c. cold water
1/2 c. boiling water
1 c. mayonnaise
1/4 c. lemon juice
1/2 c. chopped celery
1/2 c. diced green pepper
1/4 c. pickle relish
Salt and pepper to taste
1-1/2 lb. cooked, deveined shrimp
2 T. sliced pimiento

Dissolve gelatin in cold water; add boiling water. Mix with next 6 ingredients. Arrange shrimp in bottom of a 1-1/2 quart ring mold, alternating with pimiento strips. Carefully spoon remaining shrimp and gelatin mixture into mold. Chill until firm. Turn out on a bed of shredded lettuce; garnish with olives if desired. Serve with melba toast.

Roast Leg of Lamb

1 leg of lamb
1/4 t. salt
1/4 t. pepper
1/4 t. onion salt
Dash of garlic powder

Season lamb and place in a large shallow pan. Roast in preheated 300 oven for 25 minutes per pound or until oven thermometer registers 165-170.

Currant-Mint Sauce

1 glass of currant jelly
10-12 mint leaves, chopped
1/4 c. hot wine vinegar

In a pan, heat currant jelly. Pour hot wine vinegar over the chopped mint leaves. Add to melted currant jelly.

Sweet Onion Casserole

3 medium sized Vidalia onions
2 T. butter or margarine
2 4-1/2 oz. jars sliced mushrooms, drained
2 c. shredded Swiss cheese, divided
1 10-3/4 oz. can cream of chicken soup
1 5 oz. can evaporated milk
1 T. soy sauce
6 slices of 1/2" thick French bread
1/3 c. chopped fresh parsley

Cut onions in 1/4" thick slices; cut slices in half. Melt butter in a large skillet; add onion and sauté until tender. Combine onions and mushrooms in lightly greased 2 quart baking dish; sprinkle with 1 cup cheese. Combine soup, milk and soy sauce and pour over cheese. Top with bread and sprinkle evenly with remaining cheese and parsley. Cover and chill 4-8 hours or overnight. Let stand at room temperature 30 minutes. Bake, covered at 375 for 30 minutes. Uncover and bake 15-20 minutes more or until thoroughly heated. Let stand 5 minutes before serving.

Trifle

1 sponge cake
4 oz. seedless raspberry jam
8 oz. sherry
1 pint prepared egg custard
1/2 pint sweetened whipped cream
Sliced and whole almonds
Maraschino cherries

Split the cake. Spread 1 layer with the jam. Place in large bowl. Pour half the sherry on cake. Pour half the prepared custard over cake. Repeat with second layer. Store in refrigerator until next day. Just before serving add cream, nuts and cherries.

Country Ham Dinner

M E 🌼 N U

Becky Oliver, President, 1991-1993
The Garden Club of Kentucky, Inc.

Country Ham*	Biscuits*
Baked Beans*	Potato Salad*
Tomatoes	Pecan Pie*

Country Ham

18-20 lb. cured ham of 2 years old
1 c. of graham cracker crumbs
1/2 c. of brown sugar
Black pepper

Wash and trim ham. Place in lard can or ham cooker and cover with water. Cook on high temperature. Boil ham for 1 hour and 45 minutes. Cover cooker for 12 hours with blankets or other coverings. Remove ham from hot water and remove bones and skin. Wrap tightly in a clean cotton towel and tie tightly to pull meat together where bone was removed. Cool. After ham is cold, mix graham cracker crumbs, brown sugar and black pepper with enough water to make a stiff paste and cover the top of ham. Set the topping by placing ham in warm oven at 200 for about 10 minutes. Cool ham completely before slicing.

Biscuits

2 c. all purpose flour
1 c. buttermilk
1 t. baking soda
2 t. baking powder
1/3 c. shortening or lard

Mix all the ingredients and knead 30 times on a floured board.
Bake at 400ø for 15 minutes or until golden brown

Baked Beans

1 large can pork and beans
1/2 medium onion, finely chopped
1/2 c. molasses or brown sugar
1 c. ketchup

Drain bean juices in a heavy 2-quart sauce pan. Add onion, sugar
and ketchup. Cook over medium heat until onions are translucent
and sauce is thick. Add beans and simmer for about 30 minutes.

Potato Salad

1/4 c. sugar
1 T. cornstarch
1/2 c. milk
1/4 c. vinegar
1 egg
4 T. butter
3/4 t. celery seed
1/4 t. dry mustard
1/4 c. chopped onion
1/4 c. salad dressing
7 medium potatoes, cooked and diced
3 hard boiled eggs, chopped

In saucepan, combine sugar and cornstarch. Add next 6 ingredients and dash of salt. Cook over low heat until bubbly. Remove from heat and add onions and salad dressing. Cool. Add potatoes and eggs. Cool. Allow to season in refrigerator overnight.

Pecan Pie

1/2 c. butter
1 c. sugar
1/2 c. light corn syrup
1/2 c. dark corn syrup
4 eggs, beaten
1 t. vanilla
Dash salt
1 c. pecans
1 9" unbaked pie shell

Combine sugar, butter and syrups and cook over low heat until sugar is dissolved. Cool. Add eggs, vanilla and salt; blend well. Pour filling into pie shell and top with pecans. Bake at 325 for 50-55 minutes.

Pie Crust

1 c. flour
1/3 c. shortening
3 T. cold water

Mix flour and shortening until it looks like small peas. Add water and form dough ball. Roll on floured surface and put in pie pan. Set aside until pie filling is ready.

Carolyn's
Quick and Easy Summer Menu

M E 🌿 N U

Carolyn Roof, President, 1993-1995
The Garden Club of Kentucky, Inc.

Tossed Salad with Kiwi   Low Fat Italian Dressing
Steamed Summer Vegetables   Rice Pilaf
Grilled Ostrich or Bison Filets
Raspberry Sorbet with Fresh Mint

Prepare prepackaged salad greens and toss with kiwi. Top with your favorite low-fat Italian dressing purchased from the grocery.

Wash and steam summer vegetables, adding fresh dill to taste. Cook prepackaged rice pilaf and serve with grilled meat.

Buy raspberry sorbet and garnish with fresh mint. Small portions of sorbet are served to off-set the high sugar content.

This is an easy, delicious and low-fat summer menu. It is a very healthful, filling and satisfying meal. Both meats are very low in cholesterol—lower than chicken.

Dining at the Sims

M E ❦ N U

Martha Sims, First Vice President GCKY
Fleming County Garden Club

Beef Tenderloin en Croûte*
Stuffed Baked Potatoes*
Steamed Broccoli with Sauce*   Corn Pudding*
Bibb Lettuce Salad*   Tiramisù Toffee Torte*

Beef Tenderloin en Croûte

1 3-4 lb. beef tenderloin
1 pkg. frozen puff pastry sheets
1/2 lb. mushrooms, finely chopped
2 T. margarine
8 oz. cream cheese, room temperature
1/4 c. seasoned dry bread crumbs
2 T. Madeira wine
1 T. chopped fresh chives
1/4 t. salt
1 egg, beaten
1 T. cold water

Heat oven to 425. Tie meat with string at 1" intervals and place on rack in baking pan. Roast 45-50 minutes until thermometer registers 135. Remove from oven; cool 30 minutes in refrigerator. Remove string. Thaw puff pastry according to package directions. Cook and stir chopped mushrooms in skillet 10 minutes or until liquid evaporates. Add cream cheese, bread crumbs, wine, chives and salt; mix well and cool. On lightly floured surface, overlap pas-

143

try sheets 1/2" to form 14x12" rectangle; press edges firmly together to seal. Trim length of pastry 2-1/2" longer than length of meat. Spread mushroom mixture over top and sides of meat. Place meat in center of pastry. Fold pastry over meat and press edges together to seal. Decorate top with pastry trimmings, if desired. Brush pastry with combined egg and water. Place meat in a greased 15x10x1" jelly roll pan. Bake 20-25 minutes or until pastry is golden brown. Let stand 10 minutes before slicing.

Stuffed Baked Potatoes

4 large baking potatoes
1 3 oz. package of cream cheese with
a teaspoon of minced chives
3 T. butter
1/2 c. grated Parmesan cheese
2 T. sour cream
1 egg
1/2 t. salt
Dash pepper

Scrub potatoes well; grease with shortening. Bake in 400 oven for 1 hour or until fork tender. Split potatoes lengthwise and scoop out into electric mixer bowl. Add other ingredients except egg and beat until well blended. Add egg and beat until smooth. Fill potato shells and sprinkle tops with additional cheese and paprika. Bake at 375 until puffed and lightly browned.

Broccoli with Sauce

1 bunch broccoli, prepared for steaming
1 c. mayonnaise
4 T. butter
4 T. horseradish
1 small onion, grated
1/2 t. prepared mustard
1/2 t. salt
1/2 t. tabasco

Steam broccoli until desired tenderness. Mix remaining ingredients in top of double boiler. Stir until smooth. Pour over broccoli when ready to serve.

Corn Pudding

4 c. fresh corn, cut from cob
8 eggs
4 c. whipping cream
2/3 c. sugar
1-1/2 t. salt
1-1/2 t. flour
1 t. baking powder
1 T. butter, melted

Stir eggs and cream into corn. Combine dry ingredients and add to corn mixture. Stir in butter and mix well. Pour into greased baking dish and bake at 350 for an hour or until a knife inserted in the center comes out clean.

Bibb Lettuce Salad

2 heads Bibb lettuce
1 bunch fresh spinach
1 head Boston lettuce
1 head endive
1 c. corn oil
6 T. sugar
1 t. dry mustard
2 T. onion, chopped
1/2 c. apple cider vinegar
1 t. celery seed
3 oz. crumbled blue cheese
8 oz. bacon, fried

Rinse greens and drain well. Tear greens into bite-size pieces. Combine remaining ingredients, except bacon, in blender. Blend well. Crumble bacon over greens; pour dressing over and toss gently.

Tiramisù Toffee Torte

1 pkg. white cake mix
1 c. strong coffee, room temperature
4 egg whites
4 toffee candy bars, chopped
2/3 c. sugar
1/3 c. chocolate syrup
4 oz. cream cheese, softened
2 c. whipping cream
1 c. strong coffee, room temperature

Heat oven to 350. Grease and flour two 8 or 9" round cake pans. In mixing bowl, combine cake mix, 1 cup coffee and egg whites at low speed until moistened; beat two minutes at high speed. Fold in chopped candy bars. Spread batter in greased and floured pans. Bake 8" pans from 30-40 minutes or 9" pans for 20-30 minutes. Cool ten minutes and remove from pans to cool completely. In medium bowl, combine sugar, chocolate syrup and cream cheese. Beat until smooth. Add whipping cream and vanilla; beat until light and fluffy. Refrigerate until ready to use. To assemble cake, slice each layer in half to make four layers. Drizzle each cut side with 1/4 cup coffee. Place one layer coffee side up on serving plate; spread with frosting. Repeat with second and third layers. Top with remaining cake layer. Frost sides and top of cake with remaining frosting. Garnish with chopped toffee bar. Store in refrigerator.

After the Game Buffet

M E ❦ N U

Sandra Robinson, Recording Secretary,
The Garden Club of Kentucky
Lady Slippers/Laurel Garden Clubs

White Chili*
Tossed Salad with Dressing
French Bread with Butter   Chocolate Pudding Bar*

White Chili

4 chicken breast halves, skinned, boned
and cut into 1" pieces
1 15 oz. can cannelloni beans, drained
1 15 oz. can garbanzo beans, drained
1-1/2 c. water
1 11 oz. can white corn, drained
2 4 oz. cans chopped green chilies, undrained
2 chicken flavored bouillon cubes
1 onion, chopped
1 clove garlic, minced
1 t. ground cumin
1 T. vegetable oil
Hot sauce to taste
1 c. shredded Monterey Jack cheese
Fresh parsley sprigs

Combine first 7 ingredients in a 2-1/2 quart baking dish; stir well
and set aside. Sauté onion, garlic and cumin in oil in a skillet until

onion is tender. Add to chicken mixture, stirring well. Cover and bake at 350 for 50 minutes or until chicken is done. Remove from oven. Add hot sauce to taste; stir well. Sprinkle with cheese. Garnish with parsley sprigs.

Chocolate Pudding Bar

2 sticks butter
1 c. brown sugar
Self-rising flour
2 large containers Cool Whip, softened
1-1/2 c. powdered sugar
2 8 oz. pkgs. cream cheese
2 large boxes instant chocolate pudding mix
6 c. cold milk

Melt butter in saucepan. Add brown sugar and enough flour to make thick. Press into bottom of a 9x13" baking dish. Bake at 350 until lightly browned; approximately 20 minutes. Crumble and press down in baking dish. In large bowl combine Cool Whip, powdered sugar and cream cheese. Pour on top of pressed crumbs. In large bowl, pour pudding mix over milk and beat for 2 minutes. Pour on top of cheese mixture. If desired, top with cool whip and sprinkle with nuts.

Southern Favorites

M E N U

Jo Boudinot, Treasurer, The Garden Club of Kentucky
The Potted Few
Champagne and Orange Juice
Mammy Jane's Cheese and Ham*
Ambrosia Salad*   Snap or String Beans Au Vin*
Cheese Grits   Buttermilk Biscuits
Very Thin Benne Cookies*   Tipsy Squire Cake*

Mammy Jane's Cheese and Ham

6 slices white bread
3 c. baked ham, cut in bite size pieces
1/2 lb. American cheese
3 eggs
1/2 t. salt
1/2 t. paprika
1/2 t. prepared mustard
2-1/2 c. milk
1 small jar pimiento

Remove crust from bread and cut into 1" squares. In a greased casserole, alternate layers of bread, ham and cheese, ending with cheese on top. Beat eggs until frothy. Add remaining ingredients and pour over casserole. Bake at 350 for 1 hour. Serve at once. Shrimp, crabmeat or mushrooms may be added.

Ambrosia Salad

3/4 c. diced orange
2 ripe bananas, sliced
1/2 c. seedless grapes
1/4 c. pitted dates, cut up
3 T. lemon juice
1/4 c. flaked coconut
1/2 c. heavy cream
1 c. mayonnaise
Flaked coconut

Combine fruits; sprinkle with lemon juice and chill. Whip the heavy cream and fold into mayonnaise. Fold mayonnaise mixture into the fruit mixture. Serve on lettuce. Sprinkle with coconut.

Snap or String Beans Au Vin

2 lb. fresh snap or string beans
1/2 c. olive oil
2 slices thick bacon, cubed
2 medium onions, chopped
1 small clove garlic, minced
2-3 c. sauterne wine
1 T. Worcestershire sauce
Louisiana hot sauce
Salt
Water, if needed

Snap and string beans. Pour olive oil into pot large enough to hold all the beans, preferably an iron pot. Put bacon in olive oil and fry until soft, not brown. Add beans, onions, garlic and wine. Add Worcestershire sauce and Louisiana sauce, to taste. After beans become tender, add salt to taste and cook to desired doneness.

Very Thin Benne (Sesame) Cookies

3/4 c. melted butter
3/4 c. flour
1-1/2 c. light brown sugar
1 t. vanilla
1 egg
1 c. benne seeds
1/4 t. baking powder
1/4 t. salt

Mix and drop on greased pan; let it run. Bake at 375 until golden brown.   Remove from pan while hot.

Tipsy Squire Cake

1 box of frozen raspberries, strawberries or peaches
3/4 loaf pound cake, cubed
1/2 c. rum or port wine
1 box Jell-O
1 c. boiling water
1/2 c. juice from fruit
1 box instant pistachio pudding or a custard
2 c. cold milk
1/2 pint whipping cream
Chopped nuts and maraschino cherries

Defrost, drain and reserve liquid from fruit. Cube pound cake and place in clear bowl. Sprinkle cubes with rum or wine. Place fruit on top of cake.   Prepare Jell-O with boiling water and 1/2 cup reserved juice from fruit.   Pour on cake. Put in refrigerator until set. Beat pudding mix and milk for 2 minutes on low speed. Pour on top of Jell-O layer. Let set 5-10 minutes. Beat whipping cream. Smooth on top of pudding. Garnish with nuts and cherries.

A Special Occasion Brunch

M E N U

Judy Ferrell, State Headquarters Chairman,
The Garden Club of Kentucky
Bourbon County Garden Club

Brunch Sandwich*   Scalloped Tomatoes*
Steamed Asparagus   Fresh Fruit Salad
Banana Nut Bread*

Brunch Sandwich

16 slices bread, buttered with crusts taken off
8 slices sharp cheese
8 slices ham
6 eggs
3 c. milk
1/2 t. dry mustard
1/2 lb. sautéed mushrooms
1 c. crushed cornflakes
1/2 c. melted butter

Put 8 slices buttered bread on bottom of well greased 9x13" baking dish. Top each slice with cheese and ham. Put 8 slices of bread on top, buttered side up. Mix eggs, milk and mustard. Pour over bread. Refrigerate overnight. Place mushrooms on top and sprinkle with cornflakes mixed with melted butter. Bake 45 minutes at 350.

Scalloped Tomatoes

2-1/2 lb. tomatoes
2 c. fresh bread crumbs
3 T. grated onion
1 T. sugar
1 t. salt
1/2 t. pepper
3 T. butter

Cut tomatoes into thick slices and remove some of the seeds. Sprinkle 1/2 cup of the bread crumbs over the bottom of a buttered 8" square baking pan. Arrange tomato slices in pan in 3 layers, sprinkling each layer with onion, seasonings and 1/2 cup bread crumbs. Dot each layer with butter. Bake in preheated 375 oven about 30 minutes or until bubbling and browned.

Banana Nut Bread

1/2 c. butter or margarine
3 ripe bananas, mashed
1 c. sugar
2 c. flour
1 t. baking soda
2 eggs
1 c. chopped pecans

Cream butter and sugar. Add eggs. Blend thoroughly. Mash bananas and add to creamed mixture. Mix baking soda with flour. Stir into batter, add nuts. Blend all together and pour into 2 medium greased loaf pans or 4 mini loaf pans. Bake 15 minutes at 375 and turn down to 350 for 45 minutes for regular loaf pans. For mini pans, bake 10 minutes at 375 and 20 minutes at 350. Remove from pans while still warm.

O'Charley's Tomato Soup

4 T. butter
1 stalk celery, diced
1 large yellow onion, diced
5 lb. fresh tomatoes, skinned and diced
2 quarts tomato sauce
1 c. tomato paste
1/4 c. brown sugar
1/4 c. chicken base
2 t. black pepper
1 pint milk

In a large skillet, melt butter, add celery and onion. Sauté until tender. Set aside. In a large kettle bring diced tomatoes, tomato sauce and tomato paste to a simmer. Cook for 15 minutes. Add sautéed onions and celery, brown sugar, chicken base, pepper and milk. Simmer on low heat 15 minutes or until ready to serve.

Barbecue Chicken Salad Supreme

4 c. cooked and diced chicken breasts
1 8 oz. can sliced water chestnuts
2 c. celery, diced
1 t. salt
1/4 t. pepper
2 T. lemon juice
1/4 t. paprika
1 c. mayonnaise
1 c. sour cream or plain yogurt
1 c. grated cheese
Barbecue potato chips, crushed

Combine the first 9 ingredients, toss lightly. Spoon into a 9x13" baking dish. Sprinkle grated cheese and then crushed barbecue potato chips on top. Bake at 350 for 20-25 minutes, until hot and bubbly.

Cranberry Salad

2 large pkgs. raspberry Jell-O
2-1/2 c. hot water
2 cans whole cranberry sauce
1 20 oz. can crushed pineapple, undrained
1 large apple, diced small
1 c. pecans, finely chopped
1 c. celery, finely chopped (optional)
Sour cream

Pour hot water over Jell-O in large bowl. Stir until dissolved. Add whole cranberry sauce, pineapple, apple, pecans and celery. Place in a 9x13" dish and chill until firm. Cut into squares and serve on a lettuce leaf. Garnish with a dollop of sour cream.

Yeast Rolls

1 c. hot water
1 t. salt
1/4 c. sugar
1/3 c. butter
1 pkg. fast-acting yeast
2 T. lukewarm water
1 egg
Flour
Melted butter

Mix hot water, salt, sugar and butter together in a large bowl; let cool to lukewarm. Dissolve yeast in lukewarm water. Add to large bowl along with the egg and mix well. Add flour until like biscuit dough. Set in refrigerator until ready to use. On floured surface, knead and roll out 1/2" thick and cut with biscuit cutter. Dip in melted butter and place in 13x9x2" pan. Let rise until double. Bake in 400 oven for 15-20 minutes.

Mom's Pineapple Pie

3 egg yolks, slightly beaten
1/2 c. milk
1 small can pineapple
1/2 stick butter
1 c. sugar
3 T. flour

In saucepan combine egg yolks, milk, pineapple and butter; cook over medium heat, stirring constantly, until mixture comes to a boil. Mix flour and sugar together and add to milk mixture. Cook until thick. Let cool and pour into a graham cracker crust.

Graham Cracker Crust

1/2 c. butter
1/2 c. brown sugar
16 large graham crackers, rolled into crumbs, reserving 2 T.

Combine all ingredients except the reserved 2 tablespoons of graham cracker crumbs. Pat into a 9" pie plate. Bake 5 minutes. Add filling to crust, spread meringue and sprinkle with crumbs.

Meringue

3 egg whites
1/4 t. salt
6 T. sugar

Have egg whites at room temperature. Add salt; beat until frothy. Beat in sugar 1 tablespoon at a time. Beat until meringue is stiff and glossy. It is ready to spread on pie when sugar is dissolved and is stiff enough to hold a point, yet still looks moist. Bake in a slow oven until meringue is golden brown.

Ham Roll-Ups

8 slices ham
8 oz. cream cheese
1/2 c. fresh chives, finely chopped

Microwave cream cheese to spreadable consistency and add chives. Use a paper towel to absorb moisture on ham slices. Spread with cream cheese mixture. Roll in jelly roll fashion. Refrigerate for several hours before cutting in 3/4" wheel sections. Garnish with fresh parsley.

Lemon Couscous

1 T. grated lemon rind
2 T. fresh lemon juice
1 T. butter or margarine
1/8 t. salt
1 c. chicken broth
2/3 c. couscous, uncooked
3 T. fresh parsley, chopped
3 T. red bell pepper, chopped

Combine first 5 ingredients in a saucepan and bring to a boil. Add couscous, stir, cover and remove from heat. Let stand 10 minutes. Stir in pecans, parsley and bell pepper. Garnish with fresh mint sprigs.

Raspberry Bombe

1 pint whipping cream
1 c. powdered sugar
8 oz. maraschino cherries, chopped
2 t. Kirsch
1 quart raspberry sherbet
Sugared seedless grapes for garnish

Whip the cream until it holds a shape. Add powdered sugar gradually. Fold in cherries and Kirsch. Line a melon mold with 2/3 cup of cream mixture. Place mold in freezer until firm. Soften raspberry sherbet and put into mold. Cover with remaining whipped cream. Freeze overnight. Unmold with hot towels and slice. Garnish with sugared seedless grapes.

Company's Coming and It's Easy

M E N U

Jean Ohlmann,
Gardening Studies Schools Chairman, GCKY
Rambler Garden Club

Peppered Beef*	Barley Pilaf*
Fresh Roma Green Beans	Tomatoes, Cucumbers, Onions
Peppers with Herb Vinaigrette	Rhubarb Dessert*

Peppered Beef

1/4 c. coarsely ground pepper
1 t. ground cardamom
4-5 lb. boneless beef brisket
2/3 c. soy sauce
1/2 c. vinegar
1 T. catsup
1 t. paprika
3 cloves garlic, crushed

Combine pepper and cardamom on sheet of waxed paper. Place beef over mixture, press firmly with heel of hand. Repeat on other side. Combine next 5 ingredients and pour over meat in shallow dish. Cover and refrigerate overnight. Turn meat occasionally. When ready to cook, remove meat from marinade and wrap in aluminum foil. Bake in 300 oven for 3 hours. Let cool and slice across the grain. May be served with horseradish and sour cream sauce.

Barley Pilaf

1/2 c. butter
1/2 c. celery
1-1/2 c. barley
1 t. salt
1/2 c. chopped fresh parsley
2 medium onions, coarsely chopped
1/2 c. fresh mushrooms, sliced
2 c. chicken broth
1/8 t. cayenne pepper

Melt butter in skillet; stir in onions and celery. After 5 minutes, add mushrooms and sauté for 5 minutes more. Add barley and cook until light brown, stirring occasionally. Transfer to a greased 2 quart casserole. Add broth, salt, cayenne and parsley. Cover and bake about 50 minutes at 350, or until barley is tender and liquid absorbed.

Rhubarb Dessert

Crust:
1 c. sifted flour
1/2 c. butter or margarine
5 T. confectioner's sugar

Blend all ingredients together. Press into greased 9x9" square pan. Bake at 350 for 15 minutes.

Filling:
2 eggs
1/4 c. flour
1-1/2 c. sugar
3/4 t. salt
2 c. chopped rhubarb

Beat eggs; add flour, sugar, salt and rhubarb. Spoon into crust. Bake at 350 for 35 minutes. Cool. Serve with ice cream.

Dolores' Seafood Casserole

1 8 oz. pkg. egg noodles
1-1/2 lb. shrimp, shelled and cooked
1 c. fresh crabmeat or 7 oz. can
1 5 oz. can water chestnuts, drained and sliced
1/2 c. pimiento, chopped a little
4 T. butter, divided
3 T. chopped sweet onion
1/4 c. chopped green pepper
1 4 oz. can mushrooms drained and sliced
2 T. flour
3 c. light cream
1 t. salt
1/2 c. dry white wine or sherry

Cook noodles, drain and set aside. Combine seafood, water chestnuts and pimiento in a bowl. Heat 2 tablespoons butter; add onion, pepper and mushrooms. Cook until tender. Add onion mixture to seafood pan. Melt 2 tablespoons butter in same pan;

163

stir in flour and salt. Cook one minute. Remove from heat. Stir
in wine and cream gradually. Cook until it thickens slightly. Must
come to a boil. Add seafood and onion mixture. Fold in noodles.
Put in buttered casserole dish. Cook at 400 for about 45 minutes.

Rice and Spinach Pie

Pastry:
2 c. all purpose flour
1/2 t. salt
1/2 c. cold unsalted butter
2 T. shortening
1 egg
3 T. cold water

Filling:
2 10 oz. pkgs. frozen spinach
1/2 c. water
4 slices bacon
1 large sweet onion, chopped
1-1/2 c. cooked brown rice
1/2 c. shredded gruySre cheese
1 t. salt
2 pinches of ground pepper
1 t. dried basil, crushed
1/8 t. nutmeg
3 beaten eggs
2 T. butter, cut in pieces

Mix pastry and line an 8x1-1/2" round baking pan with half the
pastry. Refrigerate. Wrap the remaining pastry and trimmings in
clear plastic wrap and keep chilled for another day. Cook spinach
in water until it breaks up with a fork. Press out all excess liquid.
Set aside. Cook bacon; reserve 2 tablespoons of bacon drippings.
Remove bacon and excess drippings from pan. In reserved drippings, cook onion until tender. Add spinach, rice, cheese, salt, pep-

per, basil and nutmeg. Heat through. Stir in eggs, butter and bacon. Chill mixture for 2 hours. Fill chilled pie crust with spinach mixture. Bake 45 minutes at 375. Brush top with a mixture of beaten egg and 1 tablespoon water for a golden slick surface.

Dolores' Tossed Salad Dressing

1/2 c. vinegar
1 c. olive oil
Grated onion
Crushed garlic to taste
3 T. mustard
1 T. honey
Pinch of salt

Put all ingredients in a quart jar and shake vigorously. Will keep for many weeks.

Butterscotch Pie

2 T. butter
1 c. brown sugar
4 T. flour
Pinch of salt
3/4 C. condensed milk
3/4 C. water
2-3 egg yolks, slightly beaten
1/2 t. vanilla

Melt butter in top of double boiler. Mix sugar, salt and flour; add to melted butter. Mix well. Mix condensed milk and water together; slowly add to mixture, stirring constantly. Cook for 15 minutes after mixture becomes smooth. Add small amount of pudding to eggs and mix before adding egg yolks to hot mixture. Cook two minutes longer. Cool slightly and pour into cooked pie crust and top with your favorite meringue recipe. Brown in oven at 400.

M E ❧ N U

Romanza Johnson, Youth Chairman,
The Garden Club of Kentucky
Bowling Green Garden Club

Appetizers	Baked Fruit Dressing*
Fried Country Ham	Scrambled Eggs
Cheesy Grits	Whipping Cream Biscuits*
Bran Muffins*	Coffee Cake
Pepper Pecans*	Chocolate Pound Cake

Baked Fruit Dressing

1 15 oz. can sliced peaches, drained
1 16 oz. can sliced pears, drained
1 15-1/4 oz. can pineapple chunks, drained
1/3 c. raisins
1/3 c. chopped walnuts
3/4 c. firmly packed light brown sugar, divided
1 t. vanilla
1 15 oz. can apricot halves, drained
5 slices white bread, toasted
3/4 c. butter or margarine, melted

Combine peaches, pears, pineapple, raisins, walnuts, 1/2 cup brown sugar and vanilla; stir gently. Spoon into a lightly oiled 13x9x2" baking dish; arrange apricot halves on top. Cut bread slices into 1/2" cubes; sprinkle over fruit mixture. Combine butter and remaining 1/4 cup brown sugar; pour over bread cubes. Bake at 325 for 25-30 minutes; serve warm.

Whipping Cream Biscuits

2 c. self-rising flour
1 t. sugar
1 c. whipping cream

Combine all ingredients, mixing well; dough will be stiff. Turn out on a lightly floured surface and knead 10-12 times. Roll dough to 3/8" thickness. Cut with a 2" biscuit cutter. Place on lightly greased baking sheet. Bake at 450 for 10-12 minutes.

Bran Muffins

1 c. sugar
1/2 c. shortening
2 eggs
2-1/2 c. flour, unsifted
2-1/2 t. baking soda
1/2 t. salt
2 c. buttermilk
1 c. boiling water
1 c. 100% bran cereal
1 c. raisins
2 c. All Bran

Cream sugar and shortening. Add eggs, one at a time, beating well after each addition. Add flour, soda, salt and buttermilk, mixing until smooth. Pour boiling water over 100% bran cereal and let stand until cereal has absorbed water and cooled slightly. Blend into batter. Add raisins and All Bran, mixing thoroughly. Refrigerate. When ready to use, fill well-greased muffin tins about 2/3 full. Bake in a 400 oven for 20-25 minutes. Batter will keep covered in refrigerator up to five weeks.

Pepper Pecans

1/4 c. golden Worcestershire sauce
2 T. butter or margarine, melted
1/4 t. hot sauce
1/8 t. pepper
2 c. pecan halves

Combine first 4 ingredients in a medium bowl. Stir in pecans, and let stand 30 minutes; drain. Spread pecans in a single layer in a 13x9x2" baking pan. Bake at 250 for 35 minutes, stirring every 10 minutes. Pecans may be stored up to 2 weeks in an airtight container.

Favorite Dinner

M E  N U

Dorotha S. Oatts, President
Lexington Council, of Federated Garden Clubs

Tomato Celery Soup*
Pear Salad with Raspberry Vinaigrette*
Grilled Salmon with Jalapeño Butter*   Spinach Molds*
Sweet Potato Swirls*   Sunflower Seed Rolls
Holiday Cream Parfait*   Assorted Cookies

Tomato Celery Soup

1 small onion, chopped
1/2 c. celery, finely chopped
2 T. butter
1 10-1/2 oz. can tomato soup, diluted with 1 can water
1 t. parsley, minced
1 T. lemon juice
1 t. sugar
1/4 t. salt
1/8 t. pepper
Whipped cream

Sauté onion and celery in butter; do not brown. Add remaining ingredients and simmer for 5 minutes; the celery will remain crisp. Top each cup of soup with a spoonful of unsweetened whipped cream; garnish with additional chopped parsley.

Pear Salad with Raspberry Vinaigrette

1 c. fresh or thawed frozen raspberries
1/4 c. red wine vinegar
1/4 c. salad oil
1-2 T. sugar
1/4 t. ground cinnamon
4 C. mixed greens, torn
2 pears, cored and sliced
1 c. seedless red and green grapes, halved
1/4 c. chopped pecans

In a blender or food processor, combine raspberries and vinegar. Blend about 30 seconds or until pureed. Sieve mixture to remove seeds; discard seeds. Transfer mixture to a small bowl and stir in salad oil, sugar and ground cinnamon. Cover and chill at least 1 hour. Arrange greens, pears and grapes on salad plates. Sprinkle with pecans. Stir vinaigrette; pour over each salad.

Grilled Salmon with Jalapeño Butter

1-3/4" cube fresh ginger
2 large cloves garlic
1-2 large jalapeño peppers, seeded
1/4 c. loosely packed cilantro leaves
1/2 c. butter, softened
1-1/2 lb. fresh or frozen salmon fillets or steaks, cut 1" thick
Salt
Pepper

In a blender or food processor combine ginger, garlic and jalapeño pepper; cover and process till finely chopped. Add cilantro; cover and blend until combined. Stir into butter. On a piece of waxed paper or plastic wrap, shape butter into a 6" long log. Seal tightly and chill until serving time or freeze for up to 3 months. Sprinkle salmon with salt and pepper. Place in a well-greased grill basket or on a well-greased grill rack directly over medium coals. Grill for 8-

12 minutes. If the fish is thicker than 1", turn it halfway through cooking. When done, the fish should flake easily when tested with a fork. Place a slice of jalapeño butter atop each piece of fish.

Spinach Molds

2 10 oz. pkgs. frozen chopped spinach
1 c. frozen chopped onion
6 eggs, slightly beaten
1-1/3 c. milk
3 T. butter or margarine, melted
1-1/4 t. salt
1/4 t. pepper
1/4 t. savory
1 T. vinegar
8 tomato slices, cut 1/2" thick

Cook spinach according to directions on package; drain thoroughly. With kitchen shears, cut spinach into smaller pieces. Chop thawed onion into very fine pieces. Combine beaten eggs with milk, mix well. Combine spinach, onion, egg-milk mixture, butter, salt, pepper, savory and vinegar. Divide the mixture evenly between 8 well-greased 5-ounce custard cups. Place cups in shallow utility pan in 1" of hot water. Bake in oven at 350 for 35-40 minutes or until a silver knife comes out clean when inserted in the center of mold. Sprinkle tomato slices with salt and pepper, if desired. Loosen spinach from custard cup by running a thin spatula around edge. Lay seasoned side of tomato slice over top of custard cup and invert.

Sweet Potato Swirls

5-6 large yams or sweet potatoes
2 T. margarine or butter
2 T. frozen orange juice concentrate, thawed
1 egg
2 T. margarine or butter, melted
2 T. brown sugar

Slice 1 or 2 yams or sweet potatoes on the bias to make 8-10 1/2 "-thick slices. Cook remaining yams, covered, in boiling water for 20-30 minutes or until tender, adding unpeeled yam slices the last 10 minutes of cooking time. Drain; cool slightly. Set aside slices. Halve the whole yams lengthwise; use a spoon to scrape out pulp. Transfer the yam pulp to a large mixing bowl. Beat yam pulp with an electric mixer on low speed until yams are completely smooth. Beat in 2 tablespoons margarine or butter, orange juice concentrate and egg. Place cooked yam slices on a baking sheet. Using a decorating bag with a large star tip, pipe a decorative mound of mashed potatoes onto each slice. Drizzle with 2 tablespoons melted margarine. Sprinkle mixture with brown sugar. Bake in a 400 oven for 15-20 minutes or until heated through. Let stand 3 minutes. With a spatula, carefully transfer slices to a serving platter.

Holiday Cream Parfait

1/2 gallon vanilla ice cream, softened
1 16 oz. container frozen whipped topping, thawed
1 27 oz. jar mincemeat
2 T. cream sherry (optional)

Combine all ingredients in a large bowl, stirring until blended. Spoon mixture into parfait glasses. Cover and freeze until firm.

Fund-Raiser Buffet

M E N U

Drue LeMaster
Bourbon County Garden Club

Pork Tenderloin Marinated in Bourbon Sauce*
Henry Bain Sauce*   Horseradish Sauce
Cocktail Rolls - Yeast and Onion
Cheddar Stuffed Mushrooms*   Shrimp Mold *
Hot Artichoke Cheese Squares*
Crudités with Dill Dip   Bit of Brie Appetizer*
Lemon Squares*   Pecan Pie Brownies*

Pork Tenderloin Marinated in Bourbon Sauce

1/4 c. Kentucky Bourbon
1/4 c. soy sauce
1/4 c. brown sugar
3 cloves garlic, minced
1/4 c. Dijon mustard
1 t. fresh ginger, minced or 1/4 t. powdered ginger
1/4 c. vegetable oil
2 1-lb. pork tenderloins

Combine all ingredients, except pork, with a whisk or in a processor.   Place tenderloin and marinade in a sealable clear plastic bag in the refrigerator overnight. Cook in 350 oven 45-60 minutes or until it has just lost its pinkness. Baste while cooking. Do not overcook or it will be dry. Slice in 1/4" slices to put on cocktail rolls.

Henry Bain Sauce

17 oz. Major Grey's chutney
14 oz. catsup
14 oz. A-1 sauce
10 oz. Worcestershire sauce
12 oz. chili sauce
Tabasco sauce to taste

Mix all thoroughly. Store in glass bottles.

Cheddar Stuffed Mushrooms

2 lb. mushroom caps
8 T. butter, divided into 4 T. each
1 c. onion, chopped
1 c. soft bread crumbs
1 c. grated cheddar cheese
1/2 c. pecans
1/4 c. fresh parsley - finely chopped
1/2 t. salt
1/4 t. pepper

Clean mushrooms. Remove and chop stems, keeping caps whole; set aside.   Pour 4 tablespoons melted butter in large container and put mushroom caps in for basting. Melt 4 tablespoons butter in large skillet; add onions and stems. Sauté 2 minutes. Add remaining ingredients and stir lightly.   Spoon into caps and place in baking dish. Bake in 350 oven for 20 minutes.

Shrimp Mold

3 cans shrimp, drained
1/2 c. celery, finely chopped
1 medium onion, grated
2-1/2 pkgs. unflavored gelatin
1/3 c. cold water
1 can tomato soup, heated
4 small pkgs. cream cheese
2 c. mayonnaise
1 T. Worcestershire sauce
1 t. seasoned salt
Tabasco to taste

Beat softened cheese until fluffy. soften gelatin in water and dissolve in hot soup. Combine with cheese and beat in mixer until smooth. Fold in other ingredients. Pack into an oiled mold and chill. Unmold to serve.

Hot Artichoke Cheese Squares

1/3 c. onion, chopped
1 clove garlic, mashed
2 T. bacon drippings
4 eggs, beaten until frothy
1 14 oz. can artichoke hearts, drained and chopped;
not marinated hearts
1/4 c. dry bread crumbs
1/2 lb. Swiss cheese, shredded
2 T. minced parsley
1/2 t. salt
Pepper to taste
1/4 t. oregano
1/8 t. Tabasco sauce

Sauté onion and garlic in bacon drippings. Combine with remaining ingredients. Bake in a greased 7x11" baking dish at 325 for 25-30 minutes. Cut in 1-1/2" squares.

Bit-of-Brie Appetizer

3/4 c. pecans, finely chopped and roasted
1/4 c. coffee-flavored liqueur
3 T. brown sugar
1 14 oz. mini Brie
Apples and/or pears

Remove rind from top of Brie; discard rind. Add liqueur and sugar to pecans; stir well. Place Brie on a microwave-safe serving plate. Spoon pecan mixture over top of Brie. Microwave uncovered at high for 1-1/2 to 2 minutes or until Brie softens to desired consistency, giving dish a half-turn after 1 minute. Serve with fresh sliced apples and pears that have been dipped in fruit juice to keep from turning brown.

Lemon Squares

1 c. flour
1/4 c. powdered sugar
1 stick butter
2 eggs, slightly beaten
1 c. sugar
1 lemon, juiced
2 T. flour
1/2 t. baking powder

Cut the flour and powdered sugar into the butter until they combine to resemble fine crumbs. Press crumbs into the bottom of a 9" square baking dish. Bake 15 minutes at 300. Meanwhile, combine remaining ingredients until smooth. Pour over baked crust. Return dish to oven and bake for 25 minutes at 350. Dust with powdered sugar and cool. Cut into squares.

Pecan Pie Brownies

1/4 c. butter
2 T. flour
3/4 c. brown sugar, firmly packed
2 eggs
1 t. vanilla
2 c. pecans, chopped
2 1-1/2 oz. pkgs. fudge brownie mix

Heat oven to 350. Grease bottom of 13x9x2" pan. In medium saucepan, melt butter. Stir in flour until smooth. Add brown sugar and eggs; mix well. Cook over medium-low heat for 5 minutes, stirring constantly. Remove from heat; stir in vanilla and pecans. Set aside. Prepare brownie mix according to package directions. After spreading mix in the prepared pan, spoon filling evenly over top. Bake at 350 for 30-35 minutes or until set. Do not overbake. Cook completely. Cut into bars.

Bride's Simple But Festive Menu

M E N U

Carey Huddleston and Leora Breining
Cumberland Park Garden Club

Easy Beef Tenderloin*   Special Green Beans*
Lemon-Buttered New Potatoes*   Cold Spiced Fruit*
Commercial Rolls   Ice Cream Bombe*

Easy Beef Tenderloin

6 green onions, chopped
1/2 c. butter or margarine, melted
3 beef-flavored bouillon cubes
2 T. red wine vinegar
1 5-6 lb. beef tenderloin, trimmed

Sauté green onions in butter in a small saucepan until tender; add bouillon cubes, stirring until dissolved. Remove from heat and stir in vinegar. Place tenderloin in a large shallow dish. Spoon butter mixture over top; cover with foil and let stand at room temperature 15 minutes. Place on a rack in a roasting pan; insert meat thermometer into thickest portion. Bake at 425 for 30-45 minutes or until thermometer reaches 160 for medium or until well done. Let stand 10 minutes before slicing.

Special Green Beans

2-1/2 lb. fresh green beans
3 c. water
1 c. sliced fresh mushrooms
1/3 c. chopped onion
1 8 oz. can sliced water chestnuts, drained
1/2 t. salt
1/2 t. pepper
1/2 t. basil
1 t. dried Italian seasoning
1/3 c. olive oil
1/4 c. grated Parmesan cheese

Wash beans, trim ends and remove strings. Combine beans and water in Dutch oven. Bring to a boil. Cover, reduce heat and simmer 6-8 minutes until crisp-tender. Drain. Plunge into ice water to stop the cooking process. Drain beans and set aside. Sauté mushrooms and next 7 ingredients in oil in a Dutch oven. Stir in beans and cook until thoroughly heated. Sprinkle with Parmesan cheese.

Lemon-Buttered New Potatoes

2 lb. small new potatoes, unpeeled and quartered
1/4 c. butter or margarine
2 T. chopped fresh parsley
2 T. lemon juice
1 t. grated lemon rind
1/2 t. salt
1/4 t. pepper
1/8 t. ground nutmeg

Cook potatoes, covered, in boiling water to cover, until tender; drain carefully, leaving skins intact. Combine butter and next 6 ingredients in a small saucepan. Cook over medium heat, stirring until butter melts. Pour butter mixture over potatoes, stirring gently to coat. Garnish, if desired, with fresh parsley; serve immediately.

Cold Spiced Fruit

2 oranges, unpeeled and thinly sliced
1 t. salt
1 15-1/2 oz. can pineapple chunks, undrained
1 16 oz. can sliced peaches, undrained
1 16 oz. can apricot halves, undrained
1 c. sugar
1/2 c. white vinegar
3 3" sticks cinnamon
7 whole cloves
1 3 oz. pkg. cherry flavored gelatin

Cut orange slices in half. Combine oranges and salt in a large pan; add water to cover. Bring to a boil and cook 5 minutes. Drain well and set aside. Drain canned fruits, combining and reserving enough juice to make 2-1/2 cups, adding water if necessary. Set fruit aside. Combine juice, sugar and remaining ingredients in a medium saucepan. Bring to a boil, stirring until gelatin dissolves. Reduce heat and simmer 15 minutes. Layer fruits and orange slices in a large bowl. Pour gelatin mixture over fruit. Cover and refrigerate 8 hours or overnight. Stir and serve with a slotted spoon.

Ice Cream Bombe

1 quart vanilla ice cream, softened
1 6 oz. pkg. semi-sweet chocolate morsels
1 T. sugar
3 egg whites, at room temperature
2 t. vanilla
1/2 c. whipping cream, whipped

Garnishes:
Semi-sweet chocolate shavings,
red maraschino cherries, fresh mint sprigs.

Line a 5-cup mold with plastic wrap. Spread ice cream evenly on bottom and   sides of mold; freeze 1 hour. Combine chocolate morsels and sugar and heat over low heat until chocolate melts, stirring once. Beat egg whites and vanilla until soft peaks form. Gradually stir about 1/4 of chocolate mixture into egg whites; fold into remaining chocolate mixture. Fold in whipped cream. Spoon mixture into center of mold; cover and freeze until firm. To serve, let stand at room temperature about 10 minutes. Invert   onto a chilled serving plate. Remove plastic wrap; garnish, if desired. Return bombe to freezer until ready to serve.

Patio Brunch

M E ❦ N U

Mrs. Jefferson Caskey
Environment Chairman
Bicentennial Garden Club

Hash Brown Bake*   Fruit Cup*
Baked Tomatoes*   Easy Bran Muffins*

Hash Brown Bake

3 c. frozen shredded potatoes
1/3 c. butter or margarine, melted
1 c. finely chopped cooked ham
1 c. shredded Cheddar cheese
1/4 c. red or green bell pepper, finely chopped
2 large eggs, beaten
1/2 c. milk
1/2 t. salt
1/4 t. pepper

Thaw potatoes between layers of paper towels. Press into an ungreased 9" pie plate; drizzle with butter. Bake at 425 for 25 minutes or until lightly browned; cool on a wire rack 10 minutes. Combine ham, cheese and bell pepper; spoon into potato shell. Combine eggs and next 3 ingredients, stirring well; pour egg mixture over ham mixture. Bake at 350 for 25-30 minutes or until set. Let stand 10 minutes before serving.

Fruit Cup

1 17 oz. can apricot halves, drained
1 16 oz. can sliced peaches, drained
1 15 oz. can pineapple chunks, drained
1 11 oz. can mandarin oranges, drained
1 16 oz. can sliced pears, drained
1 16 oz. can seedless grapes, drained, or may use fresh grapes
1/2 c. orange juice
Lemon rind twist
Mint leaves

Combine the fruit, add orange juice and toss gently. Cover and refrigerate overnight. Garnish with lemon rind twist and mint leaves.

Baked Tomatoes

4 medium tomatoes, cut in half crosswise
1/8 t. pepper
1/4 t. salt
1/2 c. soft bread crumbs, toasted
3 T. chopped fresh parsley
2 cloves garlic, minced
1/4 t. dried thyme
1/4 t. dried oregano
2 T. vegetable oil

Place tomato halves in a lightly greased 12x8x2" baking dish. Sprinkle salt and pepper over the cut surface of each tomato half. Combine next six ingredients; mix well, and spoon over cut surface of each tomato. Bake at 350 for 12-15 minutes.

Easy Bran Muffins

3 c. 100% bran cereal
1 c. raisins (optional)
1 c. boiling water
2-1/3 c. all purpose flour
1-1/2 c. sugar
2-1/2 t. baking soda
1/2 t. salt
2 c. buttermilk
1/2 c. vegetable oil
2 eggs, beaten
1 c. chopped pecans

Combine cereal and raisins in a large bowl; pour water over the cereal mixture and mix well. Cool. Combine the next four ingredients. Make a well in the center of the flour mixture; add buttermilk, oil, eggs, pecans and bran mixture. Stir just enough to moisten dry ingredients. Cover and store in the refrigerator as long as one week. When ready to bake, spoon batter into greased muffin pans, filling 2/3 full. Bake at 400 for 15-18 minutes.

Viva Italia

M E N U

Donna Dunton
Bicentennial Garden Club

Antipasto Tray	Tuscan Tomato Soup
Casa D'Angelo's Salad*	Fettuccine with
	Smoked Salmon*
Ravioli*	Tiramisù*

Casa D'Angelo's Salad

1 head iceberg lettuce, torn
1 bunch romaine lettuce, torn
1 sweet red pepper, chopped
3 green onions, chopped
1/2-3/4 c. Romano and Provolone cheese, grated
1-1/2 c. Parmesan cheese, grated
1-1/2 c. Mozzarella cheese, grated
6 anchovies (optional)
8 oz. red wine vinegar
3/4 t. oregano
1-1/2 t. pepper
1 T. salt
1-1/2 t. garlic salt
1-1/4 oz. sugar
1/4 c. cornstarch
1 pint oil
Croutons
Bacon pieces

Toss first 7 ingredients in large bowl. In blender, blend anchovies, vinegar, oregano, pepper, salts, sugar and cornstarch. Pour in oil in a stream, continuing to blend until well mixed. Add dressing 15 minutes before serving. Add croutons and bacon at serving time.

Fettuccine with Smoked Salmon and Fresh Peas

1-1/2 lb. fresh or dried spinach fettuccine
2 T. olive oil
1 c. fresh peas
1/4 lb. smoked salmon, thinly sliced
1 pint heavy cream
1 T. minced shallots
2 T. white wine
Salt and pepper to taste

Cook pasta in a large kettle of lightly salted boiling water until it is al dente, or to taste. Drain and toss lightly with olive oil. Set aside in a warm place. Blanch the peas in a pot of lightly salted boiling water for 3 minutes. Drain and plunge into ice water. Drain again. Set aside. Put 4 slices smoked salmon, 2 tablespoons cream and the shallots in a blender and puree until smooth and creamy. Set aside. Bring the wine to a boil in heavy saucepan. Add the remaining cream and cook, stirring constantly, until the mixture coats the back of a spoon. Add the salmon puree and blend thoroughly. Stir over low heat until mixture is hot. Season with salt and pepper. Cut the remaining salmon into thin strips. In a large serving dish, toss the pasta with the peas and the salmon. Pour the hot sauce over it, toss well and serve immediately.

Ravioli

1 lb. ricotta cheese
2 oz. Parmesan cheese, grated
3 T. chopped parsley
1 egg
Salt and pepper to taste
Pinch of nutmeg
1 pkg. won ton wrappers

Mix all ingredients, except won ton wrappers, in a large bowl; mixing well. Put 1 won ton wrapper on a lightly floured surface, mount 1 tablespoon of the filling in the center of the wrapper and brush the edges with water. Put a second wrapper over the first, pressing down around the filling to force out the air. Seal the edges well and trim the excess dough around the filling with a decorative cutter or sharp knife. Make won ton ravioli with the remaining wrappers and filling in the same manner; transfer them as they are formed to a dry kitchen towel and turn them occasionally to let them dry slightly. Bring a kettle of boiling salted water to a gentle boil and cook the ravioli in batches for 2 minutes, or until they rise to the surface and are tender. Do not let the water boil vigorously once the ravioli have been added. Transfer the ravioli as they are cooked with a slotted spoon to a dry kitchen towel or paper towels to drain and keep them warm.

Tiramisù

4 egg yolks
2 T. sugar
1 tub mascarpone cheese
8 oz. heavy cream
2 T. brandy
Chocolate cake
Coffee liqueur

Combine egg yolks and sugar and beat until thick. Add mascarpone and whip for about two minutes. Remove and set aside. Whip the heavy cream with a pinch of sugar until it becomes whipped cream. Add brandy and mix for another minute. Fold the whipped cream with the mascarpone mix. Place in the refrigerator and let rest. Cut the cake into desired size and shape. You should have a top and bottom piece. Place bottoms on a sheet pan or cookie sheet pan, lace with the coffee liqueur. Using a pastry bag, pipe the tiramisu filling on to the cake. Repeat this with the top piece, using care when topping off the top piece. Garnish, if desired, with chocolate shavings, mint or nuts.

TOO GOOD TO MISS

The Garden Club of Kentucky, Inc.
Club Menus

"Mrs. Wallis' Christmas Party"

M E ❄ N U

The Council of Bourbon County Garden Clubs

Cranberry Tea*
Wassail Bowl
Rum Cranberry Punch
Sesame Toast Points
Cheese Straws*
Veggie Sandwiches*
Ham Spread
Ritz Cracker Cookies*
Tiger Butter*

Parisian Punch*
Williamsburg Punch
Veggie Squares
Cheese Ball
Olive Nut Spread*
Chicken Salad Sandwiches
Applesauce Strudel Bars*
Chocolate Mint Brownies*
Swedish Nuts*

Cranberry Tea

*1 pint water
Juice of one orange
Juice of one lemon
Cinnamon stick
1 t. whole cloves
1 pint cranberry juice
Sugar to taste*

Combine the first five ingredients and simmer for 15 minutes. Add the cranberry juice and sugar to taste.

Ernie Allen

Parisian Punch

2 large cans red Hawaiian Punch, chilled
1 qt. cranberry juice, chilled
1 large can frozen lemonade
1 large can frozen orange juice
1 liter bottle ginger ale, chilled

Mix together the first 4 ingredients. Pour into a punch bowl and add the cold ginger ale. If served in a punch bowl make an ice ring from 1/2 can frozen orange juice and 1/2 can water. Place this in a round mold and freeze. If served from a pitcher make ice cubes from same mixture, but add a maraschino cherry to each cube.

Mary Ann Hayes

Cheese Straws

1 c. butter
3 c. sharp cheddar cheese, grated
2 c. flour
1 t. baking powder
1 t. dry mustard
1 t. salt
1 t. red cayenne pepper
Paprika

Cream butter and cheese. Sift remaining dry ingredients, except paprika, with flour. Gradually add flour mixture to butter and cheese mixture. Add, if necessary, 1-2 tablespoons of ice water. Fill cookie press 3/4 full. Use the cookie press fitted with the star-shaped disk to shape the dough into straws. Hold press at 45 angle to cookie sheet. Starting at one end of cookie sheet, turn handle clockwise to extract dough, slowly pulling the press backward and continuing to turn handle. Pull a continuous ribbon across the cookie sheet. Repeat until cookie sheet is filled. Cut across rows every couple of inches with knife. Bake at 400 for about 10 minutes. Sprinkle with paprika while still hot from oven. Store in airtight container for up to a week or freeze them for 3 up to months.

Nell C. Collier

Olive-Nut Spread

1/2 c. pecans, chopped
1 c. stuffed olives, chopped
1 8 oz. pkg. cream cheese, softened
1/2 c. mayonnaise
2 T. olive juice

Mix all ingredients together. May be used for sandwiches or dip.

Catherine Lytle

Veggie Sandwiches

2 pkgs. crescent rolls
2 8 oz. pkgs. cream cheese, softened
1/2 pkg. Hidden Valley Ranch dressing mix
1/4 c. mayonnaise
Broccoli, carrots, cauliflower and radishes

Spread rolls on cookie sheet and pinch seams. Bake as directed. Mix together cream cheese, mayonnaise, dry Ranch dressing mix and spread this on rolls. Cut vegetables into small pieces, sprinkle on top and pat down. Refrigerate overnight, then cut into squares and serve.

Mary Ann Hayes

Applesauce Strudel Bars

1 pkg. yellow cake mix
1/2 c. margarine or butter, softened
1 t. cinnamon
1 c. applesauce
1/2 c. butterscotch chips
1/2 c. chopped nuts
1/4 c. wheat germ
1 c. powdered sugar
1/2 t. vanilla
1-2 T. milk

Heat oven to 350. In large bowl combine cake mix, margarine and cinnamon at low speed of mixer, until crumbly. Reserve 1 cup crumb mixture. Press remaining crumbs in ungreased 9x13" pan. Bake for 12 minutes. Remove from oven and spread applesauce over crust; sprinkle with butterscotch chips. In small bowl, combine reserved crumb mixture, nuts and wheat germ; mix well. Sprinkle over filling. Bake an additional 15-25 minutes or until golden brown. In small bowl, combine powdered sugar, vanilla and enough milk for desired drizzling consistency. Drizzle glaze over bars. Cool completely.

Lynn Mayfield

Ritz Cracker Cookies

1-1/2 c. chopped dates
1-1/2 c. chopped pecans
1 c. sweetened condensed milk
80-90 Ritz Crackers
8 oz. pkg. cream cheese, softened
2-1/2 c. powdered sugar
1 t. coconut flavoring

Mix first 3 ingredients and chill 3-4 hours. Spread on individual Ritz Crackers. Bake for 10-12 minutes at 350. Mix together the cream cheese, powdered sugar and coconut flavoring. Frost the cookies when cooled.

Velma Wills

Chocolate Mint Brownies

1/2 c. butter or margarine
1 c. sugar
1 t. vanilla
2 1 oz. sq. unsweetened chocolate, melted and cooled
1/2 c. flour
2 eggs
1 c. confectioner's sugar
2 T. milk
1/4 to 1/2 t. peppermint extract
Few drops green food coloring
1 oz. square unsweetened chocolate
1 T. butter

Cream butter and sugar well. Add next 4 ingredients and spread into an 8" greased square pan. Bake at 325 for 25 minutes. Mix confectioner's sugar, milk, peppermint extract and green food coloring together and chill. Spread over cooled brownies. Melt unsweetened chocolate and butter over low heat, mixing well. Pour over mint frosting, tilting pan to coat. Cut into squares.

Minnie Davis

Tiger Butter

1 lb. white chocolate or almond bark
12 oz. jar peanut butter
1 lb. semi-sweet chocolate, melted

Combine chocolate and peanut butter, then melt in a microwave or double boiler. Spread warm mixture on a waxed-paper-covered cookie sheet. Immediately pour on melted chocolate and swirl into mixture with a table knife. Cool, then cut or break in pieces.

Jean Wallen

Swedish Nuts

4 egg whites
2 c. sugar
Pinch of salt
1 lb. almonds, toasted
1 lb. pecans, toasted and salted
1/2 c. butter, melted

Beat egg whites until stiff. Gradually fold in sugar and a pinch of salt. Stir the almonds and pecans into the mixture until they are well coated. Melt the butter in a large shallow baking pan, adding the mixture of nuts. Mix all together and bake at 325, stirring every 10-15 minutes. Bake about 45 minutes until the nuts are coated and brown. Drain on paper towels.

Charlene Tate

Summer Picnic at the Lake

M E N U

Millersburg Garden Club

Country Ham   Potato Salad*
Fresh Pea Salad*   Watermelon Basket*
Italian Bread with Parsley & Chive Butter*
Texas Sheet Cake*   Iced Tea
Lemonade*

Potato Salad

5-6 medium red potatoes, cooked, peeled and cubed
1 c. chopped celery
1 small onion, chopped
1/4 c. chopped sweet pickle
4 hard cooked eggs, sliced
1 t. salt
Mayonnaise

Combine ingredients with enough mayonnaise to hold together. Chill for 2-3 hours before serving. Garnish with tomato quarters and parsley.

Fresh Green Pea Salad

3 c. fresh young peas or 2 10 oz. pkg. frozen peas, thawed
4 slices crisply cooked bacon, crumbled
1 c. sour cream or yogurt
1/4 c. chopped green onions or chives
Salt and pepper to taste
Garlic powder, fresh mint or fresh dill, as desired

Cook peas until barely tender; drain and chill. Combine all ingredients and refrigerate until ready to serve. Serve on lettuce.

Watermelon Basket

1 watermelon
Suggested fruits: *peaches, pineapple, grapes,*
blueberries, cantaloupe, honeydew melon, apples

Make a basket with a handle out of the watermelon. Placing the watermelon lengthwise, cut a basket handle from the top one-third. The remaining two-thirds of the melon becomes the basket after the pulp has been carefully removed. Save the good pieces of pulp for making watermelon balls. Cut "saw teeth" around the edge of the basket with a sharp knife. Refrigerate basket. When ready to use, fill basket with a variety of melon balls and cut-up fruits, well drained.

Parsley and Chive Butter

2 T. chopped parsley
1 T. chopped chives
8 oz. butter, softened
Juice of 1 lemon
Salt and black pepper to taste

Beat herbs in butter. Add lemon, salt and pepper. Chill well. Serve with warm bread.

Texas Sheet Cake

2 sticks margarine or butter
1 c. water
4 T. cocoa
2 c. flour
2 c. sugar
1 t. salt
1 t. baking soda
2 eggs
1/2 c. sour cream
1 stick margarine
4 T. cocoa
6 T. milk
1 c. nuts, chopped
1 lb. powdered sugar
1 t. vanilla

Bring the margarine, water and cocoa to a boil. Remove and stir in flour, sugar, salt and baking soda. Beat in eggs and sour cream. Pour into long greased cookie sheet. Bake at 350 for 20-25 minutes but no longer. Heat and melt margarine, cocoa and milk. Remove from heat and add nuts, powdered sugar and vanilla. Mix well and spread on warm cake.

Lemonade

4 c. sugar
5 c. water
Juice of 12 lemons
Juice of 4 oranges
Grated rind of 2 oranges
2 c. mint leaves

Boil sugar and water 5 minutes. Cool. Add fruit juices and rind. Pour over mint leaves. Cover. Let stand for 1 hour. Strain into jar. Keep covered in refrigerator. Use 1/3 cup syrup for each glass. Fill with crushed ice and water.

A Fleming County Feast

M E N U

The Fleming County Garden Club

Kentucky Country Ham* & Beaten Biscuits*
Scalloped Oysters*   Cheese Loaf*
Corn Pudding*   Sweet Potato Puff*
Broccoli Casserole*   Green Beans with Ham
Molded Cranberry Salad*   Seven Layer Green Salad*
Transparent Puddings*
Blackberry Jam Cake* with Caramel Icing*
Apple Crumb Pie*   Pumpkin Pie*
Ice Tea   Coffee
Brownings Apple Cider

Kentucky Country Ham

Scrub the ham well with water. Soak overnight in water to cover. The next day bring ham to a boil, slowly, on medium heat. Boil for 30 minutes, remove from the stove. Wrap heavily in blankets and/or rugs for 24 hours. Remove from water, take off skin and score. Rub with brown sugar and pepper mixed with cracker crumbs and vinegar. Brown 15 minutes in 400 oven or bake after soaking at 325 for 25 minutes per pound.

Martha Sims

Beaten Biscuits

4 c. all purpose flour
1 t. salt
1 T. sugar
2/3 c. shortening
1/2 c. milk
1/2 c. ice water

Mix together flour, salt and sugar. Cut the shortening in with a pastry blender. In a food processor, take half of the mixture at a time and add half of the milk and water. Repeat with the other half and then mix the two together. Roll out 1/4" thick. Cut out with biscuit cutter. Prick with a fork and place on ungreased cookie sheet. Bake at 325 for 20-22 minutes.

Martha Sims

Scalloped Oysters

3 c. crushed saltine crackers
2 pints fresh oysters
1 stick butter
Salt and pepper to taste
1 pint half and half
Milk, if needed

In greased casserole, layer crushed crackers and oysters, dot with butter, season with salt and pepper. Add milk to moisten crackers. Repeat layers with crushed crackers on top and enough milk to keep crackers moist. Bake 35-40 minutes in 350 oven.

Delores Craft

Cheese Loaf

1 c. milk
3 egg yolks
1 t. salt
1 T. mustard
1 T. butter
1/2 c. sugar
1/2 c. vinegar
1 lb. grated cheddar cheese
1 small can pimiento, chopped
1 c. cracker crumbs

Make a sauce of milk, egg yolks, salt, mustard, butter, sugar and vinegar.   Add the vinegar last.   Cook until thick and pour over cheese, chopped pimiento and cracker crumbs. Pour into a greased ring mold which has been sprinkled with cracker crumbs. Bake in 400 oven for 30 minutes. Let stand for 10 minutes before turning out on a platter. Fill center of ring with green peas, if desired.

Martha Sims

Corn Pudding

2 c. frozen corn
3 heaping T. sugar
2 T. flour
1 t. salt
2 eggs
2 c. milk
Cinnamon
1 stick butter, cut into pats

Grease 1-1/2 quart casserole. Mix all ingredients except cinnamon and butter. Put in prepared casserole dish and bake at 375 for 45 minutes to 1 hour. Stir occasionally, putting butter pats and cinnamon on top the last 15 minutes. Double recipe for 3 quart rectangular baking dish.

Jane Anne Clark

Sweet Potato Puff

5-6 medium sweet potatoes, peeled, cooked and mashed.
1/2 stick butter or margarine
1/4 t. salt
1 c. miniature marshmallows
1/2 t. cinnamon
1/4 t. nutmeg

Mix all ingredients together, adding more butter if needed. Spoon into casserole dish. Bake 30 minutes in 350 oven. Pecans or pineapple may be added if desired.

Delores Craft

Broccoli Casserole

4 pkgs. chopped frozen broccoli
2 sticks butter, divided
1 lb. Velveeta cheese
2 4 oz. stacks Ritz Crackers, finely crushed
Paprika

Cook broccoli in small amount of water. Drain, add 1-1/3 sticks of butter and cheese. Stir until melted. Pour into 3 quart rectangular baking dish. Top with crackers, dot with remaining butter and sprinkle with paprika. Bake at 350 for 30 minutes.

Jane Anne Clark

Molded Cranberry Salad

2 boxes cherry or raspberry Jell-O
1 pkg. cranberries
2 c. sugar
2 oranges or mandarin oranges
2 apples
1 can crushed pineapple, drained
3/4 c. chopped pecans (optional)
1 c. chopped celery (optional)

Prepare Jell-O, chill until hard enough to hold fruit. Grind berries in food chopper, add sugar to cranberries. Dice apples and oranges. Combine all ingredients. Chill until firm.

Delores Craft and Ann Griffith

Seven Layer Green Salad

1/2 head lettuce, coarsely shredded
1 c. chopped celery
1 c. chopped green pepper
1 c. chopped purple onion
1 17 oz. can small English peas, drained
1-1/2 c. mayonnaise
1-1/2 t. sugar
Grated Parmesan cheese
4 slices bacon, cooked and crumbled

Layer vegetables in the order listed in a 2 quart bowl; spread mayonnaise evenly over top. Sprinkle salad with remaining ingredients in the order listed. Cover tightly, chill 8 hours.

Delores Craft

Transparent Puddings

4 eggs, beaten with fork
2 c. sugar
2 sticks butter, not margarine
2 T. white corn syrup
2 t. vanilla
2 pkgs. tart shells

Using double boiler, cook all ingredients, except tart shells, until sugar has completely melted and you have a smooth mixture. Fill tart shells 2/3 full. Bake at 400 for about 15 minutes.

Delores Craft

Blackberry Jam Cake

1/2 c. butter or margarine
1 c. sugar
2 eggs
Pinch salt
2 c. flour
3 t. cinnamon
1 t. cloves
1 t. nutmeg
1 c. buttermilk
1 t. baking soda
1 c. blackberry jam
1 c. pecans, chopped
Raisins (optional)

Cream butter and sugar, add eggs. Mix dry ingredients. Add soda to buttermilk. Mix dry and buttermilk ingredients, beginning and ending with flour mixture. Add jam, nuts and raisins, if desired. Pour into 2 round layer cake pans or an oblong flat pan. Bake 30 minutes at 350.

Caramel Icing

1 stick butter or margarine
1 c. brown sugar
6 T. milk
1 lb. box confectioner's sugar
1 T. vanilla

Place butter, brown sugar and milk in pan over medium heat; bring to boil for 1 minute. Remove from heat, add sugar and vanilla. Beat with electric mixer until spreading consistency.

Delores Craft

Apple Crumb Pie

5-7 tart apples to make 5 cups
1 9" unbaked pie shell
1/2 c. sugar
1 t. cinnamon
1/3 c. brown sugar
3/4 c. all purpose flour
6 T. butter

Pare apples; core and cut in eighths. Arrange in unbaked pie shell. Mix 1/2 cup sugar with cinnamon; sprinkle over apples. Mix brown sugar with the flour; cut in butter until crumbly. Sprinkle over the apples. Bake at 400 for 35-40 minutes or until done. If pie browns too quickly, cover edge with foil.

Mary Ann McCormack

Pumpkin Pie

2 c. pumpkin, mashed
1/2 c. corn syrup
3 eggs
3/4 c. cream
3/4 c. brown sugar
1/2 t. salt
4 t. pumpkin pie spice (or 2 t. cinnamon and 1 t. nutmeg
1 t. pie spice)
3 T. butter
3/4 c. hot milk

Combine pumpkin, corn syrup, eggs and cream and set aside. Combine brown sugar, salt and spices and set aside. Stir together butter and hot milk. Add pumpkin and spices and mix well. Pour into crust and bake at 425 for 15 minutes and then 350 for 35 minutes.

Marti Kelly

Menu for Dinner

M E ❧ N U

Louisville Cardinal Garden Club, Inc.
Sandy Hampton

Herb-Cheese Spread*   Frosty Cranberry Tiptops*
Chicken Casserole*   Asparagus in Lemon Butter
Honey Glazed Carrots   Home Made Rolls
Hot Fudge Pie with Ice Cream*

Herb-Cheese Spread

1 t. Dijon mustard
1 12 oz. pkg. Havarti cheese
1 t. dried parsley flakes
1/2 t. freeze dried chives
1/4 t. dried whole dill weed
1/4 t. dried whole basil
1/4 t. fennel seeds
1/2 17-1/4 pkg. frozen puff pastry, thawed
1 egg, beaten

Spread mustard over top of cheese; sprinkle with parsley flakes and next four ingredients. Place cheese, mustard side down, in center of pastry. Wrap package style, trimming excess pastry. Seal seam. Place seam side down on a lightly greased baking sheet. Brush with egg; chill 30 minutes. Bake at 375 for 20 minutes; brush with egg, and bake an additional 10 minutes or until golden brown. Serve warm with assorted crackers or sliced apples or pears.

Frosty Cranberry Tiptops

1 lb. whole cranberry sauce
3 T. lemon juice
1 c. heavy cream, whipped
3 oz. whipped cream cheese
1/4 c. mayonnaise
1/4 c. confectioner's sugar, sifted
1 c. nuts, chopped
6 large paper cups

Crush cranberries with fork. Add lemon juice and pour into paper cups. Combine cream, cheese, mayonnaise, sugar and nuts. Spread over cranberries and freeze. Remove cups to serve. Nestle in a bed of greens.

Chicken Casserole

4 large chicken breasts
1 pkg. cornbread stuffing mix
2 cans cream of chicken soup
1 can cream of mushroom soup
1 stick butter

Stew chicken in water. Save chicken broth. Melt butter and mix with stuffing and 1/2 cup of the reserved chicken broth. Tear chicken into bite-size pieces. Grease 13x9" pan and cover bottom with 1/2 of the stuffing mix. Place half of the chicken pieces over stuffing mix. Dilute cream of mushroom soup with 1 can chicken broth. Pour diluted cream of mushroom soup over the chicken and stuffing in pan. Repeat layers: stuffing, then chicken. Be sure to save some stuffing for the topping. Dilute cream of chicken soup with 1 can chicken broth. Pour evenly over layers of chicken and stuffing. Sprinkle remaining stuffing over casserole. Bake at 350 for 45-60 minutes.

Hot Fudge Pie

1/2 c. butter
3 1 oz. squares unsweetened chocolate
1-1/4 c. sugar
1/4 c. flour
1/4 t. vanilla
3 large eggs
1/4 c. chopped walnuts

Melt butter and chocolate in double boiler or the microwave. Beat in sugar. Fold in flour. Add vanilla. Beat eggs, fold into chocolate mixture with nuts. Turn into a greased 9" pie pan. Bake at 350 for 20-30 minutes. Center should be moist. Do not overcook. Serve warm with ice cream.

Accent on the Derby

M E N U

Fayette County Homemakers' Garden Club
Eugenia Bell

Mint Juleps*   Frosted Strawberries
Pimiento Soup*   Stuffed Chicken Breasts en
Croûte* with Mornay Sauce*
Broccoli Casserole   Wilted Bibb Lettuce*
Blue Grass Pie*

Mint Juleps

1 c. boiling water
2 c. sugar
1/2 c. packed mint leaves
2 c. bourbon
Crushed ice
Mint sprigs, for decoration

Add sugar to boiling water and boil for 5 minutes. Cool. Add mint leaves and let brew overnight for 12 hours, stirring occasionally. Strain syrup through a fine sieve, discarding mint. Combine bourbon and syrup. Chill overnight, or until needed. Mixture should be very cold. Fill julep cups or tumblers with crushed ice; pour in chilled bourbon. Garnish glasses with mint sprigs and insert a short straw.

Pimiento Soup

4 T. butter
5 T. flour
1/2 t. salt
3 c. milk
4 c. chicken stock
1/2 c. pimiento
1/2 t. grated onion
Dash of black pepper

Melt butter. Add flour and seasoning; blend well. Add milk and chicken stock. Puree pimientos in blender and add to soup. Cook 20-30 minutes, stirring constantly, until mixture thickens.

Wilted Bibb Lettuce

4 heads Bibb lettuce
3 T. bacon or ham drippings
3 T. sugar
Salt and pepper to taste
4 T. vinegar

Cut lettuce up. Heat bacon drippings; add sugar, salt and pepper. Add vinegar carefully, as it will splatter. Pour over lettuce while hot.

Stuffed Chicken Breast en Croûte

1/2 medium onion, chopped
1/2 rib celery, chopped
1/2 carrot, chopped
1/4 c. water
1-2 chicken bouillon cubes
1/2 t. fresh chopped parsley

1/2 t. dried basil
1 tomato, peeled and chopped
1/4 t. black pepper
1/2 c. cooked rice
1/4 - 1/2 c. toasted bread crumbs
4-6 skinned boneless chicken breasts, pounded
Puff pastry, thawed if frozen
1 egg, beaten
2 T. water

Place onion, celery, carrot, water, bouillon, parsley, basil and tomato in a pot. Bring to a boil until vegetables are done. Remove from heat and stir in pepper and rice. Fold in enough bread crumbs to make mixture tight but not dry. Place stuffing in the center of each flattened chicken breast. Wrap chicken around stuffing. Place in baking dish seam side down and bake at 350 for 20 minutes, or until chicken is cooked. Cool. While breasts cook, bring pastry to room temperature, about 30 minutes. Wrap breasts in puff pastry. Beat egg with water and brush pastry. Bake at 375 until puff dough is golden brown, around 20 minutes. Place each breast on a plate and cover half with Mornay sauce.

Mornay Sauce

2 T. butter
2 T. all purpose flour
1/2 c. rich chicken stock
1/2 c. half and half
1/4 c. grated Swiss cheese
2-3 T. grated Parmesan cheese
White pepper, to taste

In a small saucepan, melt the butter. Whisk the flour until a paste forms. Cook and stir the paste for about two minutes. Slowly add the stock and half and half and heat the sauce until thickened. Stir in cheeses until they melt. Season with pepper.

Blue Grass Pie

1/2 stick butter
1/4 c. brown sugar
1/2 c. white sugar
2 T. flour
3 eggs
1/2 c. corn syrup
Pinch salt
1 t. vanilla
1/4 c. bourbon
1 c. chopped English walnuts
1 c. chocolate chips
1 9" unbaked pie shell

Heat oven to 375. Cream butter and sugars until fluffy. Add flour and mix until it is absorbed. Add eggs one at a time and mix well after each. Mix corn syrup, salt, vanilla and bourbon into batter. Fold in nuts and chocolate chips. Immediately pour into pie shell and bake 40 minutes. It should be chewy but not runny. Remove from oven and let set about 30 minutes before serving. May be rewarmed slightly, if desired, and served with vanilla ice cream.

Nuts and Bolts

3 sticks butter
3 T. Worcestershire sauce
1/2 t. garlic salt (optional)
3 t. celery salt
Few drops hot sauce
1 box Cheerios
1 box Corn Chex
1 box Rice Chex
1 box Wheat Chex
2 c. pretzel sticks
2 c. mixed nuts

Melt butter. Add Worcestershire and seasonings. Mix all ingredients in a very large baking pan. Bake at 250 for 1 hour, stirring often. Cool completely before storing.

Jodi Offutt

Vegetable Dip

1 c. mayonnaise
1 t. tarragon vinegar
1 t. horseradish
1 t. grated onion
1 t. garlic salt
1 t. curry powder
1 c. sour cream

Mix all ingredients together and chill. Serve with assorted raw vegetables.

Turnovers with Hot Pepper Jelly

1/2 c. butter
1 5 oz. sharp process cheese spread
1 c. flour
1 T. cold water
1 jar hot pepper jelly, red
1 jar hot pepper jelly, green

Cut butter and cheese into flour to form mealy texture. Sprinkle water over this and stir with fork. Shape into a ball. Cover ball with plastic wrap and refrigerate ball for 1 hour. It should be very sticky. After 1 hour, divide ball in half and put remaining half back in refrigerator. On a floured board, roll the first half to a 1/4" thickness. Cut with 3" round cookie cutter. Put green jelly in center of circle. Fold over and seal well. Roll out second ball of dough and repeat process, using red pepper jelly. Bake in 425 oven for 25-35 minutes until golden brown. Serve heated or cool.

Carolyn DeBoer

Taco Salad

1 lb. ground beef or ground turkey, browned and drained
1 1-1/4 oz. pkg. taco seasoning
1 16 oz. can cream style corn
1 16 oz. can red kidney beans, drained
1 7-1/2 oz. pkg. tortilla chips, broken
1 medium head lettuce, torn in pieces or chopped
1 medium tomato, diced
Taco sauce

Combine meat, taco seasoning, corn and kidney beans. Layer half of each in bowl: chips, meat mixture, lettuce and tomato. Repeat layers. Serve immediately with taco sauce.

Ann Fiel

Spiced Tea

3/4 c. instant tea
1 c. Tang
1 pkg. lemonade mix
1/4 c. sugar
1 t. ground nutmeg
1 t. ground cloves
2 t. ground cinnamon

Mix together and store in sealed container. Add 2-3 teaspoons per cup of hot water.

Marjorie Sweeney

Sunday Brunch
with Family and Friends
M E N U

Lady Slipper Garden Club

Mimosa　　　　Southern Chicken-Pecan Waffles*
Creole Eggs*　　　　Cornmeal Puff*
Angel Biscuits with Sliced Ham　　Asparagus Vinaigrette*
Herbed Tomatoes*
Strawberries Dipped in White & Dark Chocolate
Old Fashioned Pound Cake*　Apple-Pecan Coffee Cake*

Southern Chicken-Pecan Waffles

1/4 c. butter or margarine
1 T. chicken flavored bouillon granules
1/3 c. all purpose flour
2 c. milk
1/2 c. white wine
1 T. lemon juice
1/4 t. poultry seasoning
2 c. chopped cooked chicken
1/2 c. diced celery
2 T. chopped pimiento
1 6 oz. can sliced mushrooms, drained
1/2 c. chopped pecans, divided
6 waffles

Melt butter in a heavy saucepan over low heat; add bouillon granules and stir until blended. Add flour; cook 1 minute, stirring constantly. Gradually add milk to flour mixture; cook over medium heat, stirring constantly, until smooth. Reduce heat; stir in wine and lemon juice. Cook, stirring constantly, until thickened. Stir in next 6 ingredients, reserving 2 tablespoons pecans. Cook, stirring constantly, until thoroughly heated. Serve sauce over waffles; topped with reserved pecans.

Creole Eggs

1 large onion, chopped
1/3 c. chopped green onion
1/2 cup chopped celery
2 medium size green peppers, chopped
1/4 c. butter or margarine
1 28 oz. can whole tomatoes, undrained
1/2 t. salt
1-1/2 t. chili powder
1/2 t. pepper
1 c. thick white sauce (recipe follows)
12 hard cooked eggs, thinly sliced
1/4 c. fine, dry bread crumbs
1/4 c. grated Parmesan cheese

Sauté onion, celery and green peppers in butter in a large skillet until tender. Stir in tomatoes, salt, chili powder and pepper. Bring mixture to a boil; reduce heat. Cover and simmer, stirring occasionally, until thick, about 20 minutes. Combine tomato mixture, white sauce and eggs; stir well. Spoon into a lightly greased 2 quart casserole. Combine the bread crumbs and cheese; sprinkle over casserole. Bake at 350 for 20 minutes, or until hot and bubbly. Serve over Cornmeal Puff.

Thick White Sauce

3 T. butter or margarine
1/4 c. all purpose flour
1 c. milk
1/4 t. salt

Melt butter in a heavy saucepan over low heat; add flour, stirring until smooth. Cook 1 minute, stirring constantly. Gradually add milk; cook over medium heat, stirring constantly, until thick and bubbly. Stir in salt.

Cornmeal Puff

1 c. cornmeal
1-1/2 t. salt
4 c. milk
1 c. whipping cream
1 c. shredded Swiss Cheese, divided
Fresh parsley sprigs

Combine cornmeal and salt in a medium saucepan; stir in milk. Bring to a boil, reduce heat and simmer, stirring occasionally, until thickened, about 4 minutes. Gradually add whipping cream, stirring until smooth. Spoon half of cornmeal mixture into a lightly greased 8" square baking dish. Sprinkle 1/2 cup cheese over top. Spoon remaining cornmeal mixture over cheese. Bake at 350 for 35 minutes. Sprinkle remaining cheese over casserole; bake 5 additional minutes. Garnish with parsley.

Asparagus Vinaigrette

2 10 oz. pkgs. frozen asparagus spears
1/2 c. vinegar
1/2 c. water
2 T. chopped fresh parsley
2 T. chopped fresh chives
2 T. Dijon mustard
1/2 t. dried whole tarragon
1/2 lb. fresh spinach leaves
2 medium tomatoes, cut into wedges

Cook asparagus according to package directions; drain and place asparagus in a shallow container. Combine next 6 ingredients; mix well. Pour dressing over asparagus; chill for 3-5 hours. Place asparagus on spinach leaves and pour dressing over salad. Garnish with tomatoes.

Herbed Tomatoes

6 medium tomatoes
Salt
1/4 c. plus 2 T. fine, dry bread crumbs
1 clove garlic, minced
3 T. chopped onion
1-1/2 t. chopped fresh parsley
3/4 t. celery seeds
1/8 t. dried whole basil
1/8-1/4 t. pepper
Chopped fresh parsley

Wash tomatoes thoroughly. Cut tops from tomatoes; scoop out pulp, leaving shells intact. Chop pulp and set aside. Sprinkle salt on tomatoes; invert to drain. Combine tomato pulp and next 7 ingredients; stir well. Fill tomato shells with bread crumb mixture; sprinkle with additional parsley. Bake at 350 for 10-15 minutes.

Old Fashioned Pound Cake

2 c. butter, softened
2 c. sugar
8 eggs
3-1/4 c. all purpose flour
1/2 t. salt
2 t. vanilla extract
1 t. almond extract

Cream butter; gradually add sugar, beating until mixture is light and fluffy. Add eggs, one at a time, beating well after each addition. Combine flour and salt, stirring well; add to creamed mixture. Stir in vanilla and almond flavorings. Pour batter into a greased and floured 10" tube pan. Bake at 350 for 1 hour or until a wooden pick inserted in center comes out clean. Cool in pan 10-15 minutes; remove from pan and cool on a rack.

Apple-Pecan Coffee Cake

1/2 c. shortening
1/2 c. butter or margarine, softened
2 c. sugar
2 eggs
3 c. all purpose flour
2 t. baking powder
1 t. baking soda
1/4 t. salt
1-3/4 c. buttermilk
2 medium cooking apples, peeled and thinly sliced
1/2 c. all purpose flour
1/2 c. sugar
1-1/2 t. ground cinnamon
3 T. butter or margarine
1/2 c. finely chopped pecans

Cream shortening and 1/2 cup butter; gradually add sugar, beating until light and fluffy. Add eggs, one at a time, beating well after each addition. Combine flour, baking powder, soda and salt; add to creamed mixture alternately with buttermilk, beginning and ending with flour mixture. Spoon half of batter into a greased and floured 9x13x2" baking pan. Arrange apple slices over batter. Spread remaining cake batter evenly over top. Combine remaining flour, sugar and cinnamon, mixing well. Cut in butter with pastry blender until mixture resembles coarse meal; stir in chopped pecans. Sprinkle mixture evenly over batter. Bake at 350 for 45 minutes. Cool completely. Cut cake into squares to serve.

Potluck Picnic

M E ❦ N U

Bourbon County Garden Club

Asparagus-Artichoke Salad* Horseradish Mold*
Cheese Ball* Royal Carrot and Celery Salad*
Layered Chicken Salad* Cranberry Salad
Snappy Cheese Sandwiches*
Beaten Biscuits 'n' Ham*
Zucchini Bites* Foundation Refrigerator Rolls*
Strawberry Surprise* Peanut Butter Balls*
Kassie's Chocolate Eclair Cake Watermelon Cookies*
Double Coconut Cream Pie* Eclair Dessert*

Asparagus Artichoke Salad

2 lb. fresh asparagus
1/2 c. diced artichoke hearts in water
1/2 c. diced celery
2 T. diced white onion
1/2 c. tarragon vinegar
1 t. prepared mustard
1 T. dried dill
1 t. oregano
2-3 T. sugar
1 c. olive oil
1/2 t. garlic powder
1 t. salt
1/4-1/2 t. celery seed
Small jar chopped pimiento

Steam asparagus until tender but crisp; put in 9-1/2x13" casserole dish. Add artichokes, celery and onion. Mix remaining ingredients, pour over vegetables and marinate overnight.

Dixie Jasper

Horseradish Mold

6-1/2 pkg. lemon Jell-O
1 c. boiling water
1-1/2 T. unflavored gelatin
3 T. cold water
1 8 oz. container sour cream
1 5 oz. jar plus 2 T. horseradish
1 c. mayonnaise

Dissolve Jell-O in boiling water; soak unflavored gelatin in cold water. Combine gelatins and add remaining ingredients. Pour in a greased 1 quart mold. Unmold onto serving plate and serve with crackers.

Katie Haag

Cheese Ball

8 oz. pkg. shredded cheddar
8 oz. pkg. cream cheese, softened
2 T. margarine
2 t. pimiento, chopped
2 t. green pepper, chopped
2 t. onion, chopped
2 t. Worcestershire Sauce
1/2 t. lemon juice
Chopped pecans

Mix all ingredients together except the pecans. Form into a ball, then roll the cheese ball in the chopped pecans. Refrigerate for 8 hours or longer. Serve with crackers.

Dorcas Willis

Royal Carrot and Celery Salad

1-1/2 c. finely shredded carrots
1 c. finely chopped celery
1/2 oz. chopped walnuts
1/3 c. fat-free mayonnaise
1 t. lemon juice
2 t. sugar substitute

Mix in a medium bowl and serve on a lettuce leaf.

Jeanne Scott

Layered Chicken Salad

1 whole chicken, cooked, boned, skinned
and broken into small pieces
1 8 oz. can water chestnuts, drained and sliced
2 c. alfalfa sprouts
1 small red onion, thinly sliced
1/2 c. oil-free Italian dressing
1/2 t. ground pepper

In medium bowl, layer one-half of the following in this order: chicken, water chestnuts, sprouts and onion rings. Sprinkle with half of the dressing and half of the pepper. Repeat layers.

Nancy Litton

Snappy Cheese Sandwiches

1 lb. Velveeta Cheese or Velveeta Mexican for more zest
1 medium onion
2 T. mayonnaise
1/2 c. ketchup
1 T. Worcestershire sauce
1 T. vinegar or lemon juice
Dash of red pepper

Grind cheese and onion together. Mix with other ingredients. If not smooth, zap in the processor. Use for sandwiches, dip, fill celery or serve with crackers.

Miller Harper

Beaten Biscuits 'n' Ham

5 c. all purpose flour
1-1/2 t. baking powder
1/2 c. shortening
1/2 c. cold water
1/2 t. salt
3 T. sugar
1/2 c. milk

Mix well with dough hook until dough is smooth and blisters. Roll out, cut with beaten biscuit cutter. Bake at 350 for about 30 minutes. Easy to open while warm. Butter top half, add ham.

Waller Kenney

Zucchini Bites

1 env. golden onion soup mix
1 c. shredded Swiss cheese
2 T. grated Parmesan cheese
3/4 t. basil
1-1/2 c. shredded zucchini
1/4 c. dry bread crumbs
4 eggs, beaten

Combine all ingredients in a large bowl. Spoon mixture into well greased mini muffin pans. Bake at 350 for 20 minutes.

Emily Thompson

Foundation Refrigerator Rolls

2 c. water
1/2 c. sugar
2 t. salt
1-1/3 c. shortening
2 eggs, beaten
2 pkgs. yeast
1/4 c. lukewarm water
6 c. flour, or less
1/2 c. melted butter

Boil water, add sugar, salt and shortening. Allow to cool until lukewarm. Add eggs. Dissolve yeast in 1/4 cup lukewarm water; add to mixture . Add enough flour to make stiff dough. Place in greased bowl, cover and refrigerate until ready to use, up to 3 days ahead. Shape or roll out rolls and dip in melted butter. Place in greased pan and allow to rise until light. Bake at 375 for 15-20 minutes.

Ernie Allen

Strawberry Surprise

1 can sweetened condensed milk
1-1/2 c. water
1 3 oz. pkg. instant vanilla pudding mix
8 oz. container of Cool Whip
1 loaf size pound cake
Fruit such as strawberries, pineapple, banana

Mix milk, water and pudding and refrigerator for 5 minutes. Add cool whip. Layer in bowl a small amount of pudding mixture, pound cake and then fruit. Continue layering until all used. Garnish with strawberry slices and refrigerate.

Virginia Case

Peanut Butter Balls

2 sticks butter, melted
1/2 c. peanut butter
1 box confectioner's sugar
2-1/2 c. graham cracker crumbs
1 c. pecans, chopped
1 can flaked coconut
1 t. vanilla
1 12 oz. bag semi-sweet chocolate chips
1/4 c. paraffin

With hands mix all ingredients except chocolate chips and paraffin.
Roll out about 50 balls. Melt chips and paraffin in top of double
boiler. Using tongs, dip balls to coat. Cool.

Waller Fryman

Watermelon Cookies

1/3 c. butter or margarine, softened
1/3 c. shortening
3/4 c. sugar
1 large egg
1 T. milk
1 t. vanilla
2 c. all purpose flour
1-1/2 t. baking powder
1/2 t. salt
Red paste food coloring
1/3 c. semi-sweet chocolate mini-morsels
1-1/2 c. sifted confectioner's sugar
2 T. water
Green paste food coloring

Beat butter and shortening in a large mixing bowl at medium speed with an electric mixer. Gradually add sugar, beating well. Stir in egg, milk and vanilla. Combine flour, baking powder and salt; gradually add to cream mixture, mixing well. Add a small amount of red food coloring to color dough as desired, beating until blended. Shape dough into a ball; cover and chill at least 3 hours. Divide dough in half; store one portion in refrigerator. Roll remaining portion to 1/4" thickness on a lightly floured surface. Cut dough with a 3" round cookie cutter, cut circle in half. Place on an ungreased cookie sheet. Press several chocolate mini-morsels into each cookie. Repeat with remaining dough. Bake at 375 for 8-10 minutes. Do not brown. Cool on wire racks. Combine confectioner's sugar and water, mixing until smooth. Add a small amount of green food coloring, mixing until blended. Dip round edge of each cookie in green frosting, and place on waxed paper until frosting is firm.

Drue LeMaster

Double Coconut Cream Pie

1/3 c. sugar
1/4 c. cornstarch
1/4 t. salt
2 c. milk
1 8 oz. can cream of coconut
3 egg yolks, beaten
2 T. butter
1 c. flaked coconut
2 t. vanilla
1 baked 9" pie crust or 10 baked tart shells
3 egg whites, at room temperature
1/2 t. vanilla
1/4 t. cream of tartar
1/3 c. sugar
2 T. flaked coconut

Combine 1/3 cup sugar, cornstarch and salt. Stir in milk and cream of coconut. Cook and stir over medium heat until thickened and bubbly. Cook and stir 2 minutes more. Gradually stir about 1 cup hot milk mixture into beaten egg yolks, stirring constantly. Return to pan. Cook and stir until bubbly. Remove from heat and stir in butter. Stir in coconut and vanilla. Pour into baked pie shell or tart shells. In mixing bowl, beat egg whites, 1/2 teaspoon vanilla and cream of tartar until soft peaks form. Gradually add 1/3 cup sugar, 1 tablespoon at a time. Beat until stiff peaks form. Spread on hot filling. Sprinkle 2 tablespoons coconut over top. Bake at 350 for 15-20 minutes. Cool. Chill 3-6 hours before serving.

Cathern Lytle

Eclair Dessert

2 pkgs. French vanilla instant pudding mix
3 c. milk
1 pkg. whipped topping, mixed, or substitute Cool Whip
1 box graham crackers, whole
2 squares semi-sweet chocolate, melted
6 T. margarine
2 T. white corn syrup
1 t. vanilla
3 T. milk
1-1/2 cup confectioner's sugar

Mix pudding mix and milk and fold in whipped topping or Cool Whip. Line 9x13" pan with graham crackers. Pour 1/2 pudding on crackers; top with layer of crackers and pour remaining pudding on crackers. Top with another layer of crackers. Melt chocolate with margarine. Add corn syrup, vanilla and milk. Mix with confectioner's sugar. Pour over pan; cover with foil and refrigerate for 10 hours.

Lila Super

Entertaining the State President

M E N U

Ladies of the Limestone District

Elle Berry's Tomato Soup* Krispy Cheese Wafers*
Crunchy Romaine Toss* Sweet-Sour Dressing*
Lime Sherbet Beef Tenderloin*
Bernaise Sauce Dilled Red Potatoes
French Green Beans Ginger Glazed Carrots
Yeast Rolls Lemon Angel Pie*

Elle Berry's Tomato Soup

5 cans Campbell's Italian Tomato Soup
4 soup cans water
1 soup can Harvey's Bristol Cream

Mix all ingredients together and heat. Serve hot.

Elle Berry

Krispy Cheese Wafers

1/2 lb. sharp cheese, grated
1 stick butter, softened
1 c. flour
1/2 t. salt
Dash of hot sauce
2 c. Rice Krispies

Mix together and make into very small balls. Place on cookie sheet. Flatten balls with hands to make wafer size. Bake 7-9 minutes at 400 until slightly brown. Remove from sheet to cool.

Elle Berry

Crunchy Romaine Toss

1 c. English walnuts, chopped
1 pkg. ramen noodles, uncooked, broken up,
not using flavor pack
4 T. unsalted butter
1 bunch broccoli, chopped
1 head romaine lettuce, torn into pieces
4 green onions, chopped
1 c. sweet/sour dressing

Brown walnut pieces and noodles in butter. Cool on paper towels. Combine with chopped vegetables. Add dressing and toss.

Sweet/Sour Dressing

1 c. vegetable oil
1 c. sugar
1/2 c. white wine vinegar
3 t. soy sauce
Salt and pepper to taste

Whisk everything together. Refrigerate until cold. Whisk again and it will reach a thick consistency.

Beef Tenderloin

5-6 lb. tenderloin
Seasoned salt
Melted butter

Sprinkle meat with seasoned salt and cover with melted butter. Bake 30 minutes at 500. Remove from oven and cover with foil. Let stand at least 20 minutes.

Lemon Angel Pie

4 eggs, separated
1-1/2 c. sugar, separated
1/4 t. cream of tartar
3 T. lemon juice
1 T. grated lemon rind
1/4 t. salt
2 c. heavy cream

Beat the egg whites until foamy. Gradually add one cup of sugar and the cream of tartar. Beat until stiff but not dry. Spread on bottom and sides of a buttered 9" pie pan. Bake at 300 for 1 hour. Cool. Beat egg yolks, slightly. Stir in remaining 1/2 cup sugar, lemon juice, lemon rind and salt. Cook in top of double boiler until thickened. Cool. Whip the cream until stiff. Fold half the whipped cream into the lemon mixture and pour into meringue shell. Top with remaining whipped cream. Chill 24 hours.

Elizabeth Winn

Christmas Breakfast

M E N U

El Arbol Garden Club

Strata*   Garlic Cheese Grits*
          Hot Fruit Compote*

Strata

4 c. dry bread cubes
1 lb. bulk sausage, browned and drained
1 lb. sharp cheddar cheese, grated
1 c. green onions, sliced
1/2 c. bell pepper, chopped
8 eggs, beaten
4 c. milk
2 t. ground mustard
1/2 t. Worcestershire sauce
1/4 t. paprika
8 slices bacon, crisp and crumbled

Butter 9x13" pan. Spread bread cubes over bottom. Sprinkle sausage and then cheese, onions and bell pepper over top. Mix eggs, milk, mustard, Worcestershire sauce and paprika. Pour over ingredients in pan. Sprinkle bacon on top; cover and refrigerate overnight. Bake, uncovered, at 350 for 50-60 minutes.

Garlic Cheese Grits

6 c. water
2 t. salt
1-1/2 c. grits
1 stick butter, cut into pats
3 eggs, beaten
1 lb. cheddar cheese, grated
1-3 cloves garlic, minced

Bring water to boil with salt; gradually stir in grits with fork. Cook until water is absorbed. Stir in butter, a pat at a time. Carefully add eggs, cheese and garlic. Bake at 350 for 1 hour and 20 minutes.

Hot Fruit Compote

1 lb. pear halves
1 lb. peach halves
1 lb. pineapple slices or chunks
1 lb. apricot halves
1 large can mandarin oranges
1 small jar each red and green cherries
1/3 c. butter, melted
3/4 c. light brown sugar
Pinch curry powder (optional)
1/2 c. almonds (optional)

Drain all fruit and arrange in a 9x13" pan. Melt butter; add brown sugar and curry powder and almonds, if desired. Blend. Pour over fruit and bake at 325 for 1 hour. Refrigerate overnight and reheat.

Quick and Elegant Dinner for Guests

M E N U

Boone County Garden Club

Wild Rice & Mushroom Soup*
Parmesan Stuffed Mushrooms*
Chicken Breast Supreme*   Strawberry Spinach Salad*
Pat's Rolls*   Pineapple Wonder Cake*

Wild Rice and Mushroom Soup

1/4 c. margarine or butter
1 medium onion, diced
1 lb. mushrooms, sliced
1/2 cup celery, sliced
6 c. chicken broth, divided
1/2 c. cooked wild rice
1/2 t. salt
1/2 t. dry mustard
1/2 t. paprika
1/2 c. flour
2 c. low fat milk
3 T. dry sherry or broth

In 2 quart pot, melt butter; sauté onion, add mushrooms and celery. Sauté 2 minutes more. Add 5 cups broth, rice and spices. Simmer 5 minutes. In small bowl combine remaining broth and the flour; stir until smooth. Blend into soup and simmer until slightly thick, about 8-10 minutes. Stir in milk and sherry or broth. Heat thoroughly before serving.

Parmesan Stuffed Mushrooms

20 large fresh mushrooms
1 clove garlic, minced
1/2 c. olive oil
1/2 c. soft bread crumbs
1 T. parsley flakes
1/2 c. grated Parmesan cheese

Clean mushrooms with damp paper towels. Remove stems and chop; set aside. Sauté stems and garlic in oil until tender, remove from heat. Stir in remaining ingredients; spoon into caps. Place in shallow baking dish. Bake at 350 for 20-25 minutes.

Strawberry-Spinach Salad

Spinach leaves, washed, stemmed, chilled
3 green onions, chopped (optional)
2 c. strawberries, halved or quartered
1 orange, cut into bite size pieces
1 c. cashews, chopped
3 T. honey
1/2 t. mustard
1/2 c. salad oil
1/2 t. salt
1/2 t. paprika
2 T. vinegar

In serving bowl, combine spinach leaves, onions, strawberries, orange and cashews. In small bowl, combine honey, mustard, oil, salt, paprika and vinegar. Pour over salad when ready to serve.

Chicken Breast Supreme

1 small jar dried beef
8 chicken breasts, boned
8 strips of bacon
8 oz. sour cream
1 can cream of mushroom soup

Arrange slice of beef on each breast; roll and wrap with bacon. Arrange breasts in a greased baking dish. Combine sour cream and soup; pour over chicken. Bake uncovered at 225 for 3 hours, basting occasionally.

Pat's Rolls

1 c. sugar
1 c. shortening
1 t. salt
1 c. boiling water
2 cakes yeast
1 c. lukewarm water
2 eggs
6 c. all purpose flour

In large bowl, cream sugar, shortening and salt; add boiling water. Cool slightly. In medium size bowl, combine yeast cakes and lukewarm water. Combine with ingredients in large bowl. Add 2 eggs and mix. Gradually add flour until smooth. Place dough in a greased bowl, turning to coat both sides. Cover, let rise to double. Shape into rolls and let rise again. Bake at 375 for 15 minutes.

Pineapple Wonder Cake

1 box yellow cake mix
1 20 oz. can crushed pineapple
1-1/2 c. sugar
1 8 oz. cream cheese
1 3.4 oz. pkg. instant vanilla pudding mix
1-1/2 c. milk
3 bananas
1 8 oz. container Cool Whip
Chopped Pecans
Coconut (optional)

Bake cake mix as directed on box in a 9x13x2" glass pan. In saucepan, combine pineapple and sugar. Bring to a boil. Spread on cake while hot. In mixing bowl combine cream cheese, pudding and milk until smooth. When cake has cooled, spread cream cheese mixture over pineapple. Slice the bananas over the top. Smooth Cool Whip over and sprinkle with pecans and coconut, if desired.

INDEX

Beef

Beverages

Breads

Breakfast

24 Hour Wine and Cheese Omelet, 68
Apple Dutch Baby, 92
Bran Muffins, 167
Brunch Sandwich, 153
Cranberry Muffins, 20
Creole Eggs, 219
Dutch Baby German Pancakes, 91
Easy Bran Muffins, 184
Garlic Cheese Grits, 238
Hash Brown Bake, 182
Homer's Buttermilk Pancakes, 112
Mammy Jane's Cheese and Ham, 150
Southern Chicken-Pecan Waffles, 218
Strata, 237
Sugared Bacon, 69

Cakes

Apple-Pecan Coffee Cake, 222
Blackberry Jam Cake with Caramel Icing, 204
Craig's Pound Cake, 102
Family Brunch Cake, 70
Fresh Raspberry Chocolate Shortcake, 108
Next Best Thing to Robert Redford Dessert, 27
Old Fashioned Pound Cake, 222
Pineapple Wonder Cake, 242
Poppyseed Layer Cake, 118
Texas Sheet Cake, 199
Tipsy Squire Cake, 152

Candies

Peanut Butter Balls, 230
Tiger Butter, 196

Casseroles

24 Hour Wine and Cheese Omelet, 68
Apple Dutch Baby, 92
Bran Muffins, 167

Cookies

Desserts

Entrees

Seafood Enchiladas, 59
Shrimp Scampi, 73
Smothered Pheasant, 83
Sour Cream Green Enchiladas, 80
Stuffed Chicken Breast en Croute with Mornay Sauce, 212
Susan's Simple Chicken Salad, 29
Turkey and Ham Platters with Horseradish Sauce, 97
Venison, 54

Game

Roast Duck, 47
Smothered Pheasant, 83
Venison, 54

Lamb

Leg of Lamb with Lemon Garlic Sauce, 43
Roast Leg of Lamb with Currant-Mint Sauce, 137

Pasta

Fettucine with Smoked Salmon, 186
Ravioli, 187

Pies

Apple Crumb Pie, 206
Blue Grass Pie, 214
Blueberry Cream Pie, 21
Butterscotch Pie, 39
Butterscotch Pie, 165
Caribbean Fudge Pie, 10
Double Coconut Cream Pie, 231
Dutch Apple Pie, 51
Hot Fudge Pie with Ice Cream, 210
Lemon Angel Pie, 236
Mamo Parker's Pumpkin Pie, 50
Mom's Pineapple Pie, 157
Pecan Pie, 141

Seafood

The Gourmet Gardener

Mail to:

> *The Garden Club of Kentucky, Inc.*
> *960 Maple Grove Road*
> *London, KY 40744*

For Orders call
> *606-987-6158*

Please send me _____ copies of

The Gourmet Gardener @ $ 14.95 each _____

Postage & handling ___3.50___

Kentucky residents add 6% sales tax   @ .90 each _____

Total enclosed _____

Make check payable to The Garden Club of Kentucky, Inc.

Ship to:

NAME_____

ADDRESS_____

CITY _____STATE _____ ZIP _____

PLEASE COPY